THE LANGUAGE OF
POST-MODERN ARCHITECTURE

THE LANGUAGE OF
POST-MODERN ARCHITECTURE

THIRD REVISED ENLARGED EDITION

CHARLES A. JENCKS

CONTENTS

RIZZOLI
NEW YORK

Front cover
CHARLES MOORE (with Allen Eskew and Malcom Heard Jr. of Perez & Associates and Ron Filson), *Piazza d'Italia*, New Orleans, 1976–9. Columnar screens and flying arches lead up to one focus, the future German Restaurant with its 'Deli Order' of neon and the modern *Serliana* with raised keystone. Note the reflective glow of the neon. The dark, flat imposts, look as if they were an architect's rendering of a cross-section. (Norman McGrath).

Back cover
HANS HOLLEIN, *Austrian Travel Agency*, Vienna, 1976–8. Placed under the cool white light of a Secessionist barrel vault, which subtly mediates between different ceiling heights, are various signs of foreign travel : a bronze Lutyens dome for India, palm trees for exotic places, a ruined column for Greece and Italy, a truncated pyramid (in the corners) for Egypt. Air flight is signalled by birds, boat travel by ships' railings and theatre tickets by curtain and *Serlian* 'comic' scene. (J. Surwillo).

Frontispiece
J. V. RIGHTER, P. ROSE and P. LANKIN, *Pavilion Soixante-Dix*, St Sauveur, Canada, 1976–8. This ski lodge shows the 'double coding' characteristic of Post-Modernism, half modern with its geometric forms and flat top arch and half traditional with its Palladian exedra and false front. Some of these meanings relate to the local buildings in St Sauveur, whereas the grand gesture is appropriate for this public sport. The exedra, holding sun lamps, embraces the stage toward which the skiers aim. (Chai french).

To Maggie Keswick

First published in the United States of America in 1977 by

*R*IZZOLI INTERNATIONAL PUBLICATIONS, INC.
712 Fifth Avenue/New York 10019

Third revised and enlarged edition 1981

Library of Congress Catalog Card Number: 79-92359
ISBN: 0-8478-0288-4

Printed in Great Britain

MICHAEL GRAVES, *Portland Public Service Building*, Portland, Oregon, 1980-2. The tripartite elevation of the classical 'sky-column' with base, shaft and capital, relates this to the adjoining buildings and the American tradition of skyscrapers. Ornament and representational image are placed on an equal footing with the more purely architectural concerns of order and construction. 'Port-landia' flies on the Modernist diagonal, a symbol of the commercial aspirations to which the citizens of Portland responded just as the ancient Greeks reacted to their vulgar, running goddess — with mixed feelings. Some signs are literal, but the architecture is intended to communicate on metaphorical levels also. Architecture returns as a public as well as private art.

PREFACE

As can be seen by the images on the last thirty pages of this book we are today undergoing a classical revival of a kind. The kind is not likely to please purists, and it is certainly not Neo-Classical as it is sometimes termed in the popular press. No, the classicism is Post-*Modern*, a hybrid style relating more to the free style classicisms of 1900 than the purist approach of 1800, or having more in common with the beginning of the classical style, illustrated overleaf, than its 'classic' summation in the fifth century B.C. The reasons for this eclectic mix are not hard to find. A living language of architecture must deal with the new technologies — not only glass and steel, but also neon — as can be seen in Charles Moore's Piazza d'Italia (cover illustration). It must respond to social directions and this means both to a consumer society, with all its faults, exploitation and blatant imagery, and to pluralism. Finally, it must grow out of a previous tradition — the Modern one — even as it criticizes the recent past. All these pressures and ideals define Post-Modern Classicism, the synthesis whose commonalty was confirmed in the 1980 Venice Biennale.

One of the most interesting examples of Post-Modern Classicism will be completed in 1982 — Michael Graves' Public Service Building in Portland, Oregon. As can be seen in the above drawing, it is a mixture of styles. The base colonnade is rather Egyptian, and Italian at the same time, recalling the stripped classicism of the thirties. The shaft with its small 'eye' windows, indicating the energy crisis, and large 'face' of Slick-Tech glass has a Modern feel to it; while pilasters, indicating elevator cores within, and the flared keystone, meant to provide an anthropomorphic shape, are rather Art Deco. The top pavilions are meant to recall classical temples in a Poussin landscape, reminders of an Arcadian dream which will counteract the hard-headed packaging of real-estate within. Like much classical architecture, the Parthenon or Pompeian house, the fabric represents an ideal to be hoped for rather than one attained; the transcendence of the mundane, practical world. Here the packaging of trays of offices into the ultimate, squat, fat, ugly 'skylump' is denied by the soaring keystone, and lightened by the change of colour and surface. Here reality is overcome (or at least mediated) through the image. A Modern architect, or perhaps a Late-Modernist who used to be celebrated as a Brutalist, might have portrayed the reality in all its lumpy squalor. For Graves, however, as for other Post-Modern Classicists, the social reality which produces large bureaucratic monoliths still has a potential to express more perennial concerns: ideals of nature as seen in the topmost garden and its pavilions; ideas of civic pride and identity as seen in the statue of the local goddess of commerce — Portlandia — who flies dynamically and progressively on the Modern diagonal; ideas of urban propriety as seen in the way the building relates to its neighbours and holds the street line. What distinguishes this building, and Post-Modern Classicism at its best, is the hybrid aspect, also evident in the Temple of Artemis, overleaf. It is evidently an architecture of inclusion which takes the multiplicity of differing demands seriously: ornament, colour, representational sculpture, urban morphology — and the more purely architectural demands such as structure, space and light. The larger classical tradition, which gave birth to the more academic revivals, balanced many conflicting concerns rather than suppressed some for a simple harmony. The motivation, then as now, was to have a relevant, public art that could be partly understood.

C.J.

INTRODUCTION

This book and its long-winded title have had an unusual history which requires a little explanation. A situation has been developing in architecture over the last twenty years which is now in the process of focusing very quickly into a new style and approach. It has grown out of Modern architecture in much the way Mannerist architecture grew out of the High Renaissance — as a partial inversion and modification of the former language of architecture. This development is now generally being called Post-Modern architecture because the term is wide enough to encompass the variety of departures, and yet still indicate its derivation from Modernism. Like its progenitor the movement is committed to engaging current issues, to changing the present, but unlike the avant-garde it does away with the notion of continual innovation or incessant revolution.

A Post-Modern building is, if a short definition is needed, one which speaks on at least two levels at once: to other architects and a concerned minority who care about specifically architectural meanings, and to the public at large, or the local inhabitants, who care about other issues concerned with comfort, traditional building and a way of life. Thus Post-Modern architecture looks hybrid and, if a visual definition is needed, rather like the front of a Classical Greek temple. The latter is a geometric architecture of elegantly fluted columns below, and a riotous billboard of struggling giants above, a pediment painted in deep reds and blues. The architects can read the implicit metaphors and subtle meanings of the column drums, whereas the public can respond to the explicit metaphors and messages of the sculptors. Of course everyone responds somewhat to both codes of meaning, as they do in a Post-Modern building, but certainly with different

Above
1 DUAL CODING, *Temple of Artemis* at Corcyra, early 6th c. B.C. The typical Greek pediment shows the mixture of meanings, popular and elite, which could be read by different groups of people, on different levels. Here the running Gorgon, Medusa, with her snakes, and the rampant lion-panthers, and the various acts of murder are all represented dramatically in strong colour. This representational art literally breaks the abstract geometry at the top, but elsewhere harmony and implicit metaphor reign. Human proportions, visual refinements and a pure architecture of syntactic elements also have their place. Two different languages, each with its own integrity and audience.

intensity and understanding, and it is this discontinuity in taste cultures which creates both the theoretical base and 'dual coding' of Post-Modernism. The dual image of the Classical temple is a helpful visual formula to keep in mind as the unifying factor while different departures from Modernism are presented in this book. The buildings most characteristic of Post-Modernism show a marked duality, conscious schizophrenia.

The word Post-Modern was first put into widespread circulation in the art world, and it has become, since about 1976, a phrase applied to recent trends which go counter to orthodox Modernism (see appendix for sources). Picked up by *Newsweek* and related magazines the phrase was then applied indiscriminately to any buildings which looked different from the rectilinear boxes of the International Style. 'Post-Modern' thus meant any building with funny kinks in it, or sensuous imagery, a definition which, the reader will see, I find a bit too generous. This sense of the term, first used by Nikolaus Pevsner in his attack on the 'Anti-Pioneers', 1966, includes some sculptural decorators and confectioneers I would also condemn, but for quite different reasons than Pevsner: their buildings do not communicate coherently because they are coded exclusively on an aesthetic level. In simple terms they are misfired sculpture, unintended metaphors which are as malapropistic as Modern architecture itself (see pages 18–21).

So the term 'Post-Modern' has to be clarified and used more precisely to cover, in general, only those designers who are aware of architecture as a *language* — hence one part of my title. Paul Goldberger and a few American critics have used the term this way and focused on other important qualities; its attention to historical memory and local context. These aspects are significant, but as the last chapter shows, they are only part of the story. For Post-Modern architecture also takes a positive approach towards metaphorical buildings, the vernacular, and a new, ambiguous kind of space. Hence only a plural definition will capture its many heads, something I have tried to clarify with the evolutionary tree on page 80, and the history of the tradition in the last chapter. For the same reason, there is no one architect who altogether combines these various strands, or one building which summarises them. If forced to point at an entirely convincing Post-Modernist I would instance Antonio Gaudí, obviously not a possibility, as reviewers were quick to point out, because he was a Pre-Modernist. The first edition of this book ended with his work since it used a rich language so convincingly to communicate important meanings, but now I have cut out this section for reasons of space and consistency. I still regard Gaudí as *the* touchstone for Post-Modernism, a model with which to compare any recent buildings to see if they are really metaphorical, 'contextual' and rich in a precise way, but have confined my examples to the present.

The ambiguity of the prefix 'Post' has its amusing and powerful aspects, which partly explain why it has become current. People are naturally exhilarated at the prospect of being 'Post-Present'. In the middle sixties Daniel Bell wrote on the Post-Industrial Society, with the implication that some fortunate Westerners could escape laborious toil altogether. There was the short-lived 'Post-Painterly Abstraction', a movement of opposition as it states, and more recently President Carter has come out in favour of a new foreign policy based on the 'Post-War' world. Very convenient this slippery word, it simply states where you've left, not arrived.

But the mind rebels at all this linguistic paradox: how can we be beyond the modern age if we're still alive? Have we banished the present tense like the Futurists and located Elysium in a perpetual state of tomorrow (or yesterday)? If so we might look forward to a 'Post-Natal', or is it 'Post-Coital' depression, as we reap the benefits of evading the present.

Such thoughts made me consider Post-Modern architecture a temporary label when I first used it in 1975, but now I've changed my mind. Partly this is due to those overtones of 'modern' which are still kept in the hybrid title; its power and contemporaneity. Architects, artists, people in general want to keep up to date, even if they don't want to relinquish their cultural past as the avant-garde has often done. We can see in the Renaissance an instructive parallel when the word 'modern' was first put into currency.

At that time they had debates, and confusions, similar and relevant to our own. Filarete, for instance, claimed he 'used to like modern (*scil.*, Gothic) buildings' until the time 'when I began to appreciate classical ones, I came to be disgusted with the former . . .' But then as the *renaissance* of antiquity proceeded, the Gothic style became old-fashioned and, finally with Vasari, the equation was reversed: the older, classical style was perfected, that is to say *improved* (or so they thought) as the new, 'good modern style' (*buona maniera moderna*). Thus Renaissance writers were confused over the use of this term, *moderna* was applied to the Gothic, the classical Roman and its revival — three different modes. No matter how committed to the past the architects were they still called it 'modern', as if the term had (and still has?) an unchallengeable hold on the present tense — on being 'now'. Only after Giorgio Vasari systematically and consciously used *moderna* to mean the revival style did his usage become common and accepted.

The battle of the 'Ancients and Moderns' has been fought many times since then with equal confusion in usage, and in a sense we are again in such a predicament with the adversaries not only disagreeing, but also using their basic words differently. This is not the place to analyse differing versions of 'the modern', an analysis which I'm sure will occur as the attacks and counter-attacks mount in vehemence. But it is the point to em-

2 MORRIS LAPIDUS, *Eden Roc Hotel,* Miami, 1954. Lapidus started the Ersatz styling of large hotels with his confections during the fifties in Florida. He mixes all the popular periods of interior design — Louis XIV, Robert Adam, Moderne Streamlined — in a distinctive but unclassifiable style. This one is 'it-could-be-Baroque'. Lapidus came to this commercial formula through shop designs, and now it has been applied with success throughout the world — as the following London hotels show. (Morris Lapidus Associates, Architects).

phasise that the word 'modern' still has an ambiguous power, as it did for Vasari, because it refers to a contemporaneous, growing climate of opinion, and it has this power even for those who would deny, refute or criticise it. Post-*Modernism* thus gains some of these overtones even while it attacks the concept of the avant-garde and the *Zeitgeist*.

Secondly, and more importantly, the label describes the *duality* of the present situation quite well. Most, if not all, the architects of the moment have been trained in Modernism yet have moved beyond or counter to this training. They have not yet arrived at a new synthetic goal, nor have they given up entirely their Modernist sensibility, but rather they are at a half-way house, half Modern, half Post. If we look at Venturi, Stern or Moore's work — three of the hard-core PMs — we can see all the quotes from Le Corbusier, Kahn, the twenties *and* all the references to Palladio, Lutyens and Route 66. There is no doubt such work is schizophrenically coded, something you'd expect *after* a movement has broken down and the architects have moved on. For we are talking here of an evolution out of or away from a shared position, not a revolutionary schism with the immediate past, and so one of the really surprising, even defining, characteristics of Post-Modernism emerges: it includes Modernist style and iconography as a potential approach, to be used where this is appropriate (on factories, hospitals and a few offices). Whereas Modernism like Mies van der Rohe was exclusivist, PM is so totally inclusive as to allow even its purist opposite a place when this is justifiable. Put another way, Post-Modernism is finding a rationale for twenties revivalism, in an era when all revivals are possible and each depends on an argument from *plausibility*, since it certainly can't be proved as necessary.

Modern architecture suffered from elitism. Post-Modernism is trying to get over that elitism not by dropping it, but rather by extending the language of architecture in many different ways – into the vernacular, towards tradition and the commercial slang of the street. Hence the double-coding, the architecture which speaks to the elite and the man on the street. It's of course not a very easy way to design at first, before the dualism becomes conventionalised. But when a tradition grows from this base, like the classical Greek mentioned at the outset, it can be much richer and more dynamic than a pure elitism. Why? Because it can speak to other architects, the professional elite who care about and can make fine discriminations in a fast-changing language, *and* it can speak to the users who want beauty, a traditional ambience and a particular way of life. Both groups, often opposed and often using different codes of perception, have to be satisfied. And architecture, which has been on an enforced diet for fifty years, can only enjoy itself and grow stronger and deeper as a result.

All the above helps explain this new edition and why there is a new last chapter which outlines the tradition of PM as it developed from the fifties. Previously I had con-centrated on the 'language' of my title, something Geoffrey Broadbent pointed out, and now I hope the other part is more adequately represented. But I don't claim a definitive treatment to this continuing discussion and look forward to other books on the subject, one by Robert Stern which is under way, an issue of *The Harvard Architecture Review*, and an exhibition at MOMA – soon to be rechristened the Museum of Post-Modern Art (following Douglas Davis *et al*).

As I acknowledged previously, I owe a debt of gratitude to Conrad Jameson for clarifying my views and reading the text. Even more than before I now see his uncompromising advocacy of past models, pattern books based on vernacular, as a challenge to Modernism and Post-Modernism, although I find the implications reductive and too restrictive. And again my thanks go to Maggie Keswick whose opinions changed and sharpened so many of my own, and to her the dedication of the book, for being tenacious about clearing up some matters of style and some of the more unlovable prose.

Also I'm grateful for the efforts Haig Beck and Jackie Cooper have expended on the text, the former for having initiated and criticised the book and the latter for going way beyond the call of duty and reading it, slowly, backwards – to cut out hidden typographical errors. Lastly I am thankful to Andreas Papadakis who has kept an interest in the book and encouraged this new version.

Appendix

The first use of Post-Modern in an architectural context that I am aware of is way back in 1949, and by Joseph Hudnut, in an article, 'The Post-Modern House' from *Architecture and the Spirit of Man*, Cambridge, 1949, republished in Lewis Mumford's *Roots of Contemporary American Architecture*, Reinhold Publishing Corp., New York, 1952. As Penny Sparke pointed out, in a review of the first edition of this book (*Artscribe No. 8*), Nikolaus Pevsner used the phrase 'post-modern style' – but he only used it once, and then to attack those he also called 'Neo-Expressionist'. Since these architects, by and large, do not treat architecture as a language, nor use it to communicate intended meanings, I would call them Late Modernists, rather than Post-Modernists (see my text above). Pevsner's 'Architecture in Our Time, The Anti-Pioneers' was published in *The Listener*, December 29, 1966, and January 5, 1967.

Newsweek used the term ('Rise of the Come-Hither Look', January 17, 1977) to refer to the new faceted glass towers in America with their sleek, sensuous surfaces – otherwise not distinguishable from Modern ones. Paul Goldberger, in articles on Charles Moore, Hardy, Holzman and Pfeiffer and others has used it to refer to an architecture which is rich in symbolism and historical allusion. In conversation, February 1977, he stressed the importance of the picturesque image – something I find rather too wide and marginal as a definer. Drexler also questioned, in conversation, his application of the term to HHP. See Goldberger's pieces in the *New York Times* Sunday Magazine, January 16, 1977, February 20, 1977, etc.

I first used the term in April 1975 and then at a seminar in Eindhoven; see *Architecture-inner Town Government*, Technische Hogeschool, Eindhoven, July, 1975, pp. 78–103 for my article 'The Rise of Post-Modern Architecture', later reprinted in the *AAQ* issue on the subject, London, Number 4, 1975. Further articles were 'The Revisionists of Modern Architecture' concerned with a day of the RIBA Conference in July 1976, published in *Architecture: Opportunities, Achievements*, edited by Barbara Goldstein, RIBA Publications, London, 1977, pp. 55–62. The issue of *Architectural Design*, April 1977, is devoted to the subject and there I discuss the genealogy of the tradition, pp. 269–271. Finally, an article in *The Sunday Times*, May 27, 1977, pp. 30–1, 'More Modern than Modern', illustrates three aspects of Post-Modernism (participation, ornament and city pluralism).

Joseph Rykwert, in a sense similar to Pevsner, used the term 'post-Modern Movement style' in 'Ornament is No Crime', *Studio International*, September 1975, p. 95.

Erwin Panofsky discusses uses of the terms *moderna* etc. in his *Renaissance and Renascences in Western Art* (1960), from where these quotes are taken. See the Paladin edition, London, 1970, pp. 19–21, 33–35.

The Harvard Architecture Review plans its first issue on Post-Modernism in early 1978, and Arthur Drexler foresees an exhibition on the subject in February 1979, at the Museum of Modern Art.

C. Ray Smith uses the term in his *Supermannerism, New Attitudes in Post-Modern Architecture*, E. P. Dutton, New York, 1977, but just in his title. He treats several of the American architects also considered here. Various lecture series on Post-Modernism were put on at Yale, IAUS New York, UCLA. Columbia, in 1976.

PART ONE
The Death of Modern Architecture

Happily, we can date the death of modern architecture to a precise moment in time. Unlike the legal death of a person, which is becoming a complex affair of brain waves versus heartbeats, modern architecture went out with a bang. That many people didn't notice, and no one was seen to mourn, does not make the sudden extinction any less of a fact, and that many designers are still trying to administer the kiss of life does not mean that it has been miraculously resurrected. No, it expired finally and completely in 1972, after having been flogged to death remorselessly for ten years by critics such as Jane Jacobs; and the fact that many so-called modern architects still go around practising a trade as if it were alive can be taken as one of the great curiosities of our age (like the British Monarchy giving life-prolonging drugs to 'The Royal Company of Archers' or 'The Extra Women of the Bedchamber').

Modern Architecture died in St Louis, Missouri on July 15, 1972 at 3.32 p.m. (or thereabouts) when the infamous Pruitt-Igoe scheme, or rather several of its slab
3 blocks, were given the final *coup de grâce* by dynamite. Previously it had been vandalised, mutilated and defaced by its black inhabitants, and although millions of dollars were pumped back, trying to keep it alive (fixing the broken elevators, repairing smashed windows, repainting), it was finally put out of its misery. Boom, boom, boom.

Without doubt, the ruins should be kept, the remains should have a preservation order slapped on them, so that
4 we keep a live memory of this failure in planning and architecture. Like the folly or artificial ruin — constructed on the estate of an eighteenth-century English eccentric to provide him with instructive reminders of former vanities and glories — we should learn to value and protect our former disasters. As Oscar Wilde said, 'experience is the name we give to our mistakes', and there is a certain health in leaving them judiciously scattered around the landscape as continual lessons.

Pruitt-Igoe was constructed according to the most progressive ideals of CIAM (the Congress of International Modern Architects) and it won an award from the American Institute of Architects when it was designed in 1951. It consisted of elegant slab blocks fourteen storeys high with rational 'streets in the air' (which were safe from cars, but as it turned out, not safe from crime); 'sun, space and greenery', which Le Corbusier called the 'three essential joys of urbanism' (instead of conventional streets, gardens and semi-private space, which he banished). It had a separation of pedestrian and vehicular traffic, the provision of play space, and local amenities such as laundries, crèches and gossip centres — all rational substitutes for traditional patterns. Moreover, its Purist style, its clean, salubrious hospital metaphor, was meant to instil, by good example, corresponding virtues in the inhabitants.

Good form was to lead to good content, or at least good conduct; the intelligent planning of abstract space was to promote healthy behaviour.

3 MINORU YAMASAKI, *Pruitt-Igoe Housing,* St Louis, 1952–55. Several slab blocks of this scheme were blown up in 1972 after they were continuously vandalised. The crime rate was higher than other developments, and Oscar Newman attributed this, in his book *Defensible Space,* to the long corridors, anonymity, and lack of controlled semi-private space. Another factor: it was designed in a purist language at variance with the architectural codes of the inhabitants.

4 PRUITT-IGOE AS RUIN. Like the Berlin Wall and the collapse of the high-rise block, Ronan Point, in England, 1968, this ruin has become a great architectural symbol. It should be preserved as a warning. Actually, after continued hostilities and disagreements, some blacks have managed to form a community in parts of the remaining habitable blocks — another symbol, in its way, that events and ideology, as well as architecture, determine the success of the environment.

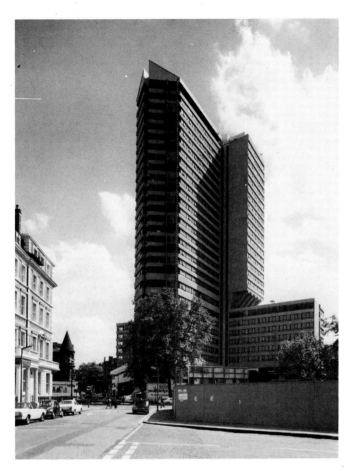

5 RICHARD SEIFERT, *Penta Hotel*, London, 1972. The English government subsidised these kinds of hotels in the late sixties to cope with the tourist boom. Twenty or so, with about 500 bedrooms, sprang up on the main route in from the airport. On the outside they are uptight International Style, on the inside Lapidus Ersatz. (R. Seifert & Partners).

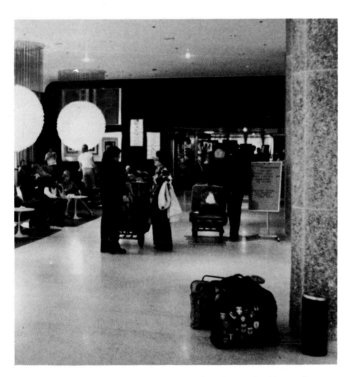

6 PENTA HOTEL, interior themed in the Vassarely-Airport-Lounge style. The irony that the same interiors could be found where the tourist left home has not escaped many critics. Nonetheless this tradition continues to thrive.

Alas, such simplistic ideas, taken over from philosophic doctrines of Rationalism, Behaviourism and Pragmatism, proved as irrational as the philosophies themselves. Modern Architecture, as the son of the Enlightenment, was an heir to its congenital naivities, naivities too great and awe-inspiring to warrant refutation in a book on mere building. I will concentrate here, in this first part, on the demise of a very small branch of a big bad tree; but to be fair it should be pointed out that modern architecture is the offshoot of modern painting, the modern movements in all the arts. Like rational schooling, rational health and rational design of women's bloomers, it has the faults of an age trying to reinvent itself totally on rational grounds. These shortcomings are now well known, thanks to the writings of Ivan Illich, Jacques Ellul, E. F. Schumacher, Michael Oakshott and Hannah Arendt, and the overall misconceptions of Rationalism will not be dwelt upon. They are assumed for my purposes. Rather than a deep extended attack on modern architecture, showing how its ills relate very closely to the prevailing philosophies of the modern age, I will attempt a caricature, a polemic. The virtue of this genre (as well as its vice) is its license to cut through the large generalities with a certain abandon and enjoyment, overlooking all the exceptions and subtleties of the argument. Caricature is of course not the whole truth. Daumier's drawings didn't really show what nineteenth-century poverty was about, but rather gave a highly selective view of *some* truths. Let us then romp through the desolation of modern architecture, and the destruction of our cities, like some Martian tourist out on an earthbound excursion, visiting the archaeological sites with a superior disinterest, bemused by the sad but instructive mistakes of a former architectural civilisation. After all, since it is fairly dead, we might as well enjoy picking over the corpse.

Crisis in architecture

In 1974 Malcolm MacEwen wrote a book of the above title which summarised the English view of what was wrong with the Modern Movement (capitalised, like all world religions), and what we should do about it. His summary was masterful, but his prescriptions were wildly off the mark: the remedy was to overhaul a tiny institutional body, the Royal Institute of British Architects, by changing a style here and a heart there — as if these sorts of things would make the *multiple causes* of the crisis go away. Well, let me make use of his effective analysis, not his solution, taking as a typical grotesque of modern architecture one building type: modern hotels.

The new Penta Hotel in London has 914 bedrooms, 5 which is almost nine times the average large hotel of fifty years ago, and it is 'themed' (a word of decorators) in the International Style and a mode which could be called Vassarely-Airport-Lounge-Moderne. There are 6 about twenty of these leviathans near each other, on the way to the London Airport (it is known in the trade as 'Hotellandia'), and they create a disruption in scale and city life which amounts to the occupation of an invading army — a role tourists tend to fulfil.

These newly formed battalions with their noble-phoney names include The Churchill (500 bedrooms, named after 7 Sir Winston and themed in the Pompeian-Palladian Style by way of Robert Adam); the Imperial Hotel (720 bedrooms, International outside, fibreglass Julius Caesar inside); and the Park Tower (300 bedrooms, themed in 8 Corn-on-the-Cob and various sunburst motifs inside).

7 The CHURCHILL HOTEL, London, 1971. A typical combination of revival style with modern services. The brochure reads : 'Your car glides to a stop under the cover of the *porte cochère*. The door is opened. Your fleeting glance sees faces . . . uniforms . . . a hand touching a hat brim in half salute . . . good evening, sir . . . this way, please . . . and you enter the lobby. Before you stretches a hall. Cool and distant and almost white. Crystal chandeliers bathe the marble floors and columns in soft white light. There are people but it is rather quiet. Composed feelings. And elegant. This is the Churchill.' If Robert Adam only had air-conditioners and down lighters he might have achieved something as cool and distant too.

8 RICHARD SEIFERT, *The Park Tower*, London, 1973. Compared to a gaso-metre, stacked television sets, and corn-on-the-cob, this modelled exterior was an attempt to get away from the flat facade. The interior is themed with the stock-in-trade sunburst motif. (R. Seifert & Partners).

A recurring aspect of these hotels, built between 1969 and 1973, is that they provide very modern services, such as air-conditioning, themed in old-world styles which vary from Rococo, Gothic, Second Empire, to a combination of all three styles together. The formula of ancient style and modern plumbing has proved inexorably successful in our consumer society, and this Ersatz has been the major commercial challenge to classical modern architecture. But in one important way, in terms of architectural *production*, Ersatz and modern architecture contribute equally to alienation and what MacEwen calls 'the crisis'. I have tried to untangle the different causes of this situation, at least eleven in number, and show how they operate in the two modern modes of architectural production (listed in the two right hand columns of the diagram).

For contrast, the first column on the left refers to the old system of *private* architectural production (operating largely before World War One) where an architect knew his client personally, probably shared his values and aesthetic code. An extreme example of this is Lord Burlington's Chiswick Villa, an unusual situation where the architect was the builder (or contractor), client and user all at once. Hence there was no disparity between his rather elite and esoteric code (a spare, intellectual version of the Palladian language) and his way of life. The same identity exists today, although on a more modest scale and as a relative rarity — the 'Handmade Houses' which are built outside urban centres in America, or the boat house community in Sausalito, in San Francisco Bay, where

9 AIR-CONDITIONING at the *Elizabetta Hotel*
1972. The incorporation of many modern services — electric candelabra, muzak, surveillance systems, telephone, alarm bell, elevators — within Ersatz styles produces incongruous juxtapositions. A surreal humour is sometimes sought, although underplayed. The ingenuity is undeniable, and some hotels, like the Elizabetta, have the courage of their own vulgarity.

10 'CRISIS IN ARCHITECTURE' a diagram of three systems of architectural production. The left column shows the implications of the old, private system of production, while the right columns show the two modern systems. Critics of modern architecture have emphasised several of these eleven causes of the crisis, but clearly the causes are multiple and work as a *system* tied into the economic sphere. The question is — how many variables must be changed for the system to change?

		SYSTEM 1 — PRIVATE private architect / client is user		SYSTEM 2 — PUBLIC public architect / client and users differ		SYSTEM 3 — DEVELOPER developer architect / client and users differ	
1	ECONOMIC SPHERE	Mini-Capitalist (restricted money)		Welfare-State Capitalist (lacks money)		Monopoly-Capitalist (has money)	
2	MOTIVATION	aesthetic ideological	inhabit use	solve problem	user's housing	make money	make money to use
3	RECENT IDEOLOGY	Too various to list		progress, efficiency, large scale, anti-history, Brutalism, etc.		Same as System 2 plus pragmatic	
4	RELATION TO PLACE	local architect	client user in place	remote architects	users move to place	remote and changing draughtsmen	absent clients
5	CLIENT'S RELATION TO ARCHITECT	Expert Friend same partners small team		Anonymous Doctor changing designers large team		Hired Servant doesn't know designers or users	
6	SIZE OF PROJECTS	"small"		"some large"		"too big"	
7	SIZE/TYPE OF ARCHITECT'S OFFICE	small partnership		large centralised		large centralised	
8	METHOD OF DESIGN	slow, responsive, innovative, expensive		impersonal, anonymous, conservative, low cost		quick, cheap, and proven formulae	
9	ACCOUNTABILITY	to client-user		to local council and bureaucracy		to stockholders, developers and board	
10	TYPES OF BUILDING	houses, museums, universities, etc.		housing and infrastructure		shopping centres, hotels, offices, factories, etc.	
11	STYLE	multiple		impersonal safe, contemporary, vandal-proofed		pragmatic cliché and bombastic	

each boat house is built by the inhabitant in a different, personalised style. These self-built houses testify to the close correspondence there can be between meaning and form when architectural production is at a small scale and controlled by the inhabitant.

Other factors which influenced this type of production in the past include the *mini-capitalist economy* where money was restricted. The architect or speculative builder designed relatively *small* parts of the city at one go; he worked *slowly*, responding to well-established needs, and he was *accountable* to the client, who was invariably the user of the building as well. All these factors, and more that are shown in the diagram, combined to produce an architecture understood by the client and in a language shared by others.

The second and third columns refer to the way most architecture is produced today and show why it is out of scale with historic cities, and alienating to both architects and society. First, in the economic sphere, it's either produced for a public welfare agency which lacks the money necessary to carry out the socialist intentions of the architects, or it is funded by a capitalist agency whose monopoly creates gigantic investments and correspondingly gigantic buildings. For instance, the Penta Hotel is owned by the European Hotel Corporation, a consortium of five airlines and five international banks. These ten corporations together create a monolith which by financial definition must appeal to mass taste, at a middle-class level. There is nothing inherently inferior about this taste culture; it's rather the economic imperatives determining the size and predictability of the result which have coerced the architecture into becoming so relentlessly pretentious and uptight.

Secondly, in this type of production, the architect's motivation is either to solve a problem, or in the case of the developer's architect, to make money. Why the latter motivation doesn't produce effective architecture as it did in the past remains a mystery, (unless it is connected with the compelling pressures of predictable taste). But it is quite clear why 'problems' don't produce architecture. They produce instead 'rational' solutions to oversimplified questions in a chaste style.

Yet the greatest cause of alienation is the *size* of today's projects: the hotels, garages, shopping centres and housing estates which are 'too big' – like the architectural offices which produce them. How big is too big? Obviously there is no easy answer to this, and we await the detailed study of different building types. But the equation can be formulated in general, and it might be called 'the Ivan Illich Law of Diminishing Architecture' (parallel to his discoveries of counter-productive growth in other fields). It could be stated as follows: 'for any building type there is an upper limit to the number of people who can be served before the quality of the environment falls'. The service of the large London hotels has fallen because of staff shortages and absenteeism, and the quality of tourism has declined because the tourists are treated as so many cattle to be shunted from one ambience to the next in a smooth and continuous flow. Programmed,

11 SAUSALITO BAY BOAT HOUSES, 1960– . Like the Handmade Houses of California, these boat houses depend on the oldest form of architectural production – *self-build*. Each one is tailor-made by the inhabitant in a different style, and you find cheek-by-jowl, a Swiss chalet boat house and a converted caravan, or here, the Venturi style next to the A-frame Fuller style.

12 PENTA RESTAURANT interior with its royal, fibreglass cartouche *Dieu-et-mon-droit*. Actually Holiday Inns, the biggest multinational in hotels, prefabricates these fibreglass symbols and then sends them out to some of their 1,700 concessions. The multinationals have been instrumental in standardising world taste and creating a world 'consumption community'. The National Biscuit Company foresees the goal of two billion biscuit munchers eating their standard average cookie.

13 DISNEYLAND, opened in 1955 as a dream of Walt Disney, started the new form of ride-through parks where people are put on a continuously moving assembly line and then shunted past 'experiences'. Sometimes the ride is effortless and you aren't aware of the mechanisms. At other times long queues form and you are ushered into people pens. Multinationals, such as Pepsi, Ford, General Electric and Gulf, have heavily invested in Disney Enterprises.

continuously-rolling pleasure, the shunting of people into queues, pens and moving lines, a process which was perfected by Walt Disney, has now been applied to all areas of mass tourism, resulting in the controlled bland experience. What started as a search for adventure has ended in total predictability. Excessive growth and rationalism have contradicted the very goals that the institution of tourism and planned travel was set up to deliver.

The same is true of large architectural offices. Here design suffers because no one has control over the whole job from beginning to end, and because the building has to be produced quickly and efficiently according to proven formulae (the rationalisation of taste into clichés based on statistical averages of style and theme). Furthermore, with large buildings such as the Penta, the architecture has to be produced for a client whom no one in the office knows, (that is, the ten corporations), and who is, in any case, not the user of the building. In short, buildings today are nasty, brutal and too big because they are produced for profit by absentee developers, for absentee landlords for absent users whose taste is assumed as clichéd.

There is, then, not one cause of the crisis in architecture, but a *system of causes*; and clearly to change just the style or ideology of the architects, as is proposed by many critics, isn't going to change the whole situation. No amount of disaffection for the International Style or Brutalism, for high-rise, bureaucracy, capitalism, gigantism, or whatever else is the latest scapegoat is going to change things suddenly and produce a humane environment. It would seem we have to change the whole system of architectural production at once, all eleven causes together. And yet perhaps such a radical move is not necessary. Perhaps some causes are redundant, some are more important than others, and we only have to change a

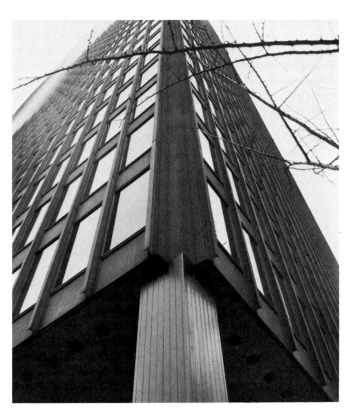

15, 16 MIES VAN DER ROHE, *Seagram Building,* New York, 1958. Corner detail and plan. The plane of I-beams is extended out a few inches from the column line so that the corner is clearly articulated with angles of steel. The interior curtains now can only be raised to pre-selected, harmonious positions. Mies kept full-scale I-beam details by his desk to get the proportions just so. He thought this member was the modern equivalent of the Doric column, but as Herbert Read once said: 'In the back of every dying civilisation sticks a bloody Doric column'.

14 MIES VAN DER ROHE, *Lake Shore Drive Housing,* Chicago, 1950. The first classic use of the curtain wall sets the formula for further variations which Mies pursued to the end of his life. Here the black steel facade line is without depth and the curtains behind the glass are allowed a random setting – 'problems' which Mies later 'solved'. The greater problem, that housing looks like offices, was never raised. (John Winter).

combination of a few. For instance, if large architectural offices were divided into small teams, given a certain financial and design control, and put in close relation to the ultimate users of the building, this might be enough. Who knows? Experiments must be tried with different variables. All that can be said at this point is that the situation has systemic causes which have to be varied as a structure if deep changes are to be made. I will pursue only two causes of the crisis: the way the modern movement has impoverished architectural language on the level of form; and has itself suffered an impoverishment on the level of content, the social goals for which it actually built.

Univalent form

For the general aspect of an architecture created around one (or a few) simplified values, I will use the term **univalence**. No doubt in terms of expression the architecture of Mies van der Rohe and his followers is the most univalent formal system we have, because it makes use of few materials and a single, right-angled geometry. Characteristically this reduced style was justified as rational (when it was uneconomic), and universal (when it fitted only a few functions). The glass-and-steel-box has become the single most used form in modern architecture, and it signifies throughout the world 'office building'.

Yet in the hands of Mies and his disciples this impoverished system has become fetishised to the point where it overwhelms all other concerns (in a similar way the leather boot dominates the shoe fetishist and distracts him from larger concerns). Are I-beams and plate glass appropriate to housing? That is a question Mies would dismiss as irrelevant. The whole question of appropriateness, 'decorum', which every architect from Vitruvius to Lutyens debated, is now rendered obsolete by Mies' universal grammar and universal contempt for place and function. (He considered function as ephemeral, or so provisional as to be unimportant.)

14   His first, classic use of the curtain wall was on housing, not for an office – and obviously not for functional or communicational reasons, but because he was obsessed by perfecting certain formal problems. In this case, Mies concentrated on the proportion of the I-beam to panel,
15,   set-back, glass area, supporting columns and articulating
16   lines. He kept full-scale details of these members close to his draughting board so he'd never lose sight of his loved ones.

A larger question thus didn't arise: what if housing looked like offices, or what if the two functions were indistinguishable? Clearly the net result would be to diminish and compromise both functions by equating them: working and living would become interchangeable on the most banal, literal level, and unarticulated on a higher, metaphorical plane. The psychic overtones to these two different activities would remain unexplored, accidental, truncated.

Another masterpiece of the modern movement, the
17   Chicago Civic Center, designed by a follower of Mies, also shows these confusions in communication. The long horizontal spans and dark corten steel express 'office building', 'power', 'purity', and the variations in surface express 'mechanical equipment'; but these primitive (and occasionally mistaken) meanings don't take us very far. On the most literal level the building does not communicate its important civic function; nor, more importantly, the social and psychological meanings of this very significant

17 C. F. MURPHEY, *Chicago Civic Center,* 1964. In terms of Mies' curtain wall this solution shows the horizontal emphasis – long spans and underplayed verticals in brown, especially rusted steel. Except for the Picasso sculpture out front, you would not recognise the civic importance of this building, nor the various political functions that occur within. (Hedrich-Blessing).

building task (a meeting place for the citizens of Chicago).

How could an architect justify such inarticulate building? The answer lies in terms of an ideology which celebrates process, which symbolises only the changes in technology and building material. The modern movement fetishised the means of production, and Mies, in one of those rare, cryptic aphorisms that is too hilarious, or rather delirious, to let pass, gave expression to this fetish.

I see in industrialization the central problem of building in our time. If we succeed in carrying out this industrialization, the social, economic, technical, and also artistic problems will be readily solved. (1924)[1]

What about the theological and gastronomic 'problems'? The bizarre confusion to which this can lead is shown by Mies himself in the Illinois Institute of Technology campus in Chicago, a large enough collection of varied functions for us to regard it as a microcosm of his surrealist world.

Basically, he has used his universal grammar of steel I-beams along with an infill of beige brick and glass to speak about all the important functions: housing, assembly, classrooms, student union, shops, chapel, and so forth. If we look at a series of these buildings in turn we can see how confusing his language is, both literally and metaphorically.

A characteristic rectangular shape might be deciphered 18 as a teaching block where students churn out one similar idea after another on an assembly line – because the factory metaphor suggests this interpretation. The only

18 MIES VAN DER ROHE, *Siegel Building, IIT,* Chicago, 1947. Is this an astrophysical research lab? The whole campus is in the 'universal' aesthetic of steel, glass and beige brick, except for the most important building. (*See* 22).

19 THE INFAMOUS IIT CORNER of the previous building. The corner looked like a full *visual* stop to Leslie Martin, yet Llewelyn-Davies argued it looked 'endless' because it was stepped back with two I-beams and an L-beam. The fact that the whole building signified 'factory', when it was for teaching, was typically overlooked in this fetish for details and esoteric meaning.

20 MIES VAN DER ROHE, *IIT Cathedral/Boiler House,* Chicago, 1947. The traditional form of a basilica with central nave and two side aisles. There are even clerestory lights, a regular bay system and campanile to show that this is the cathedral.

recognisable sign in the building, the lattice-work disc at the top, suggests that the students are budding astro-physicists; but of course Mies cannot claim credit for this bit of literalism. Someone else added it, destroying the purity of his fundamental utterance. What he can claim credit for, and what has exercised great architectural debate, (a debate between two English deans, Sir Leslie Martin and Lord Llewelyn-Davies), is his solving of the
19 *problem* of the corner. These two schoolmen disputed, with medieval precision and inconsequentiality, whether the corner symbolised 'endlessness', or 'closedness' like a Renaissance pilaster. The fact that it could symbolise both

or neither, depending on the code of the viewer, or the fact that larger questions of factory symbolism and semantic confusion were at stake — such questions were never raised.

Not so far away from this disputatious corner is another architectural conundrum, designed in Mies' universal 20 language of confusion. Here we can see all sorts of con-ventional cues which give the game away: a rectangular form of cathedral, a central nave structure with two side aisles expressed in the eastern front. The religious nature of this building is heightened by a regular bay system of piers; it's true there are no pointed arches, but there are

21 MIES VAN DER ROHE, *IIT Boiler House/Church.* A dumb box placed to either side of high-rise buildings, which are in the same vernacular. Blank on three sides and lit by a search light – clearly this is the boiler house.

22 MIES VAN DER ROHE, *IIT President's Temple/School of Architecture,* Chicago, 1962. The black temple hovers miraculously from a giant order of steel trusses and a minor order of I-beams. The white horizontal steps also break the law of gravity. The building occupies a major point on the campus, as the President's house should. (John Winter).

clerestory windows on both aisle and nave elevations. Finally, to confirm our reading that this *is* the campus cathedral, we see the brick campanile, the bell tower that dominates the basilica.

In fact, this is the boiler house, a solecism of such stunning wit that it can't be truly appreciated until we see the actual chapel, which looks like a boiler house. This is an unassuming box in industrial materials, sandwiched balefully between dormitory slabs with a searchlight attached – in short, signs which confirm a reading of prosaic utility.

Finally, we come to the most important position on the campus, the central area, where there is a temple constructed in a homogeneous material that distinguishes it from the other factories. This temple is raised on a plinth, it has a magnificent colonnade of major and minor orders, and a grandiose stairway of white marble planes miraculously hovering in space, as if the local god has ultimately worked his magic. It must be the President's house, or at very least, the Administration Centre. Actually it's where the architects work – what else could it be?

So we see the factory is a classroom, the cathedral is a boiler house, the boiler house is a chapel, and the President's temple is the School of Architecture. Thus

17

23 FRANK LLOYD WRIGHT, *Marin County Civic Center,* San Rafael, California, 1959–64. The great *Pont du Gard* made out of cardboard, gilt and golden bauble, surmounted by an Aztec minaret, with interior bowling-alleys of space, and a baby-blue, opaline roof with cookie-cutter hemi-circles. An excellent piece of Kitsch modern, unfortunately unintended.

24 I. M. PEI, *Everson Museum,* Syracuse, New York, 1968. Hardly communicative as a museum. It might be a warehouse, four theatres, or a church, except that the blank box with funny shapes became *the* sign of museums in America by 1975. By stressing sculptural consistency above all other values, Pei's work becomes surreal and reduced in significance.

25 I. M. PEI, *Christian Science Church Center,* Boston, 1973. Very hard-edge Le Corbusier – in fact Chandigarh done with precision concrete. From the air you can appreciate the fact that this centre is laid out like a giant phallus which culminates, appropriately, in a fountain. Ledoux designed a phallus-planned building as a brothel, but there is no further indication here that some elaborate message is intended.

Mies is saying that the boiler house is more important than the chapel, and that architects rule, as pagan gods, over the lot. Of course Mies didn't intend these propositions, but his commitment to reductive formal values inadvertently betrays them.

Univalent formalists and inadvertent symbolists

Lest we think Mies is a special case, or somehow uncharacteristic of modern architects in general, let us look at similar examples which stem from the reaction against his particular language: the formalist reaction in America and the Team Ten critique in Europe both turned against the Miesian approach in the sixties.

23   Frank Lloyd Wright's last work, the Marin County Civic Center, is characteristic of the formalist architecture. The building is based on the endless repetition of various patterns (and their transformation), which are uncertain in their overtones – in this case the baby-blue and golden

baubles reminiscent of a Helena Rubenstein ambience, and superimposed arches associated with a Roman aqueduct. The arches belie their compression function and hang, with gilded struts, in tension. A golden minaret-totem-pole, which also has Aztec and Mayan associations, crowns the site of this city centre (which is missing only its city). In defence one can applaud its compelling, surrealist image, justifiable in terms of its kitsch extravagance, but not much more. Like the Chicago Civic Center already mentioned, it doesn't tell us anything very profound about the role of government (escapism?) or the citizens' relation to it.

If we look at the work of I. M. Pei, Ulrich Franzen, Philip Johnson or Skidmore, Owings and Merrill, the leading American architects, we find the same erratic signification – always a striking form, a reduced but potent image, with unintended meanings. For instance, Gordon Bunshaft's museum for the Hirschhorn Collection,

26 SKIDMORE, OWINGS and MERRILL, Bunshaft designer, *Bieneke Library,* Yale University, 1964. This pompous temple looks extraordinary at night when the light shines through the translucent marble: the panels look like stacked television sets which have all gone on the blink. (US Information Service).

27 GORDON BUNSHAFT and SOM, *Hirschhorn Museum,* Washington DC, 1973. Symbolism at its most inadvertent – a concrete pillbox meant to protect art from the people? A marble doughnut? (Hirshhorn Museum).

the only collection of modern art on the Mall in Washington, is in the very powerful form of a white masonry
27 cylinder. This simplified shape, ultimately stemming from the eighteenth-century 'modernists', Boullée and Ledoux, was meant to communicate power, awe, harmony and the sublime. And so it does. But, as *Time* magazine and other journals pointed out, it symbolises more accurately a concrete bunker, a Normandy pillbox, with its battered walls, impenetrable heaviness, and 360 degree machine-gun slit. Bunshaft is inadvertently saying 'keep modern art from the public in this fortified stronghold and shoot 'em down if they dare approach'. So many cues, in such a popular code, reinforce this meaning and make it obvious to everyone not retrained in the architects' code. It might have been a multivalent statement of this meaning had the architect really intended it and combined the pillbox image with further cues of an ironic nature. But, as with the unintended witticisms of Mrs Malaprop, all credit for humour must go to the subconscious.

Aldo Rossi and the Italian Rationalists try very sympa-
28, 29 thetically to continue the classical patterns of Italian cities, designing neutral buildings which have a 'zero degree' of historical association; but their work invariably recalls the Fascist architecture of the thirties – despite countless disclaimers. The semantic overtones are again erratic, and focus on such oppressive meanings, because the building is oversimplified and monotonous. Serious critics and apologists for them, such as Manfredo Tafuri, find themselves evading the obvious in their attempt to justify such buildings with elaborate, esoteric interpretation.[2]

29 GUERRINI, LAPADULA and ROMANO, *Palace of Italian Civilisation, Eur,* Rome, 1942. Deflowered classicism and endlessly repeated blank forms. This is the architecture of control, and some future study may show how it depends on boring redundancy for its coercion.

28 ALDO ROSSI, *The Gallaratese Neighbourhood,* Milan, 1969–71. A long portico of repeated piers is surmounted by endlessly recurring rectangular windows. The interior corridors are also barren funnels of emptiness. Because the forms are 'empty' some critics have assumed they are above historical associations; but the signs are conventional and the meanings are quite well established in Italy.

30 HERMAN HERTZBERGER, *Old Age Home,* Amsterdam, 1975. An intricate puzzle of small-scaled elements, a human scale in the details. But this is multiplied to vast proportions. The incessant symbolism of white crosses containing black coffins is equally unpremeditated and unfortunate.

This disparity between popular and elitist codes can be found everywhere in the modern movement, especially among the most highly acclaimed architects, such as James Stirling, Arata Isozaki, Ricardo Bofill and Herman Hertzberger. The better the modern architect, the less he can control obvious meanings. Hertzberger's Old Age Home is, on a sophisticated level, the delightful casbah he intended, with many small-scale places and a closely-grained urban fabric where the individual is psychologically hidden and protected by the nooks and crannies. As an abstract piece of form it communicates humanism, care, intricacy and delicacy. That is the Chinese puzzle quality of the various interlocked elements and spaces acquire these meanings by analogy. Yet such subtle analogy is hardly enough when more potent, metaphorical meanings have run amok. For what are the obvious associations of this Old Age Home? Each room looks like a black coffin placed between white crosses (in fact a veritable war cemetery of white crosses). Despite his humanism, the architect is inadvertently saying that old age, in our society, is rather fatal.

Ah well, these 'slips-of-the-metaphor' are committed more and more by the top modernists, and they can even be made by architects who see architecture as a language — by Peter and Alison Smithson. It is interesting that, like other apologists for the modern movement since 1850, they justify their work in terms of the linguistic analogy,

31 ARATA ISOZAKI, *Gunma Prefectural Museum*, Takasaki, 1974. A dramatic sequence of spaces is disciplined by aluminium squares and grids everywhere. But the technocratic overtones are unsympathetic to certain kinds of fine art exhibited inside, and the overall expression is limited to a single range of meanings: precision, order, and the pervasive hospital metaphor so common in modern architecture. (Masao Arai/Japan Architect).

and look to previous languages of architecture for their lesson. They say of the city of Bath: 'it's unique . . . for its remarkable cohesion, *for a form language understood by all . . . contributed by all*'.[3] Their analysis of this Georgian city of light and dark stonework shows it to have a wide relevant language, a consistent language, from humble details such as street grills, to grand gestures such as porticoes. These porticoes the Smithsons characterise as **metaphors** for large doors, and pediments as metaphors for cheaper doors – in short, they are acutely aware of the way architectural language depends on *traditional* symbolism.

This makes their own anti-traditionalism all the more poignant and bizarre; but the Smithsons, as veritable descendants of the Romantic Age, must 'make it new' each time to avoid the censure of conventionality. Thereby, of course, they successfully avoid communicating, for all developed languages must contain a high degree of conventional usage, if only to make innovations and deviations from the norm more correctly understood.

When speaking about a possible modern language, Peter Smithson comes down firmly like a 1920s modernist in support of a machine aesthetic.

   . . . for the machine-supported present-day cities, only a live, cool, highly controlled, rather impersonal architectural language can deepen that base-connection, make it resonate with culture as a whole.[4]

The fallacies of this position are well known, yet many architects today are still committed to such notions because of their training in processes of production, and their ideology of progress. They still believe in a *Zeitgeist*, and one determined by machinery and technology – so the buildings they produce symbolise these now somewhat old-fashioned demons.

The great irony is, however, that they also believe in providing essentially humanist values of 'place, identity,

33 ALISON and PETER SMITHSON, *Robin Hood Gardens,* London, 1968–72. Unrelieved concrete (except for curtains), popularly identified now with the image of an industrial *process.* The variations of vertical fins are not strong enough to identify each apartment. The packed-in scale gives the feeling of there being a dense human wall.

32 JOHN WOOD II, *Royal Crescent,* Bath, 1767–80. One of the first examples of housing treated as a palace – the coliseum was another model. Although making a grand urban gesture, the individual houses still have an identity, marked by vertical separation and several variations in articulation (chimneys, fire walls, fences). The Smithsons are acutely aware of this symbolism, which makes their failure to provide its equivalent all the more poignant. (Bath City Council).

34, 35 SMITHSONS, *Robin Hood Gardens,* street in the air, and collective entry. The long empty streets in the air don't have the life or facilities of the traditional street. The entry ways, one of which has been burned, are dark and anonymous, serving too many families. The scheme has many of the problems which Oscar Newman traced to a lack of defensible space. Here architectural critic Paul Goldberger mimes an act that often occurs.

personality, home-coming', (I am quoting from several Team Ten sources, values which the Smithsons share). How can you communicate these meanings if you use a new language based on the machine metaphor? It would be very hard, practically impossible, and the Smithsons haven't yet pulled off this miracle. Their Robin Hood Gardens, in the East End of London, simply does not do the trick.

Robin Hood Gardens is not a modern version of the Bath Crescent, in spite of the large urban gesture and V-shaped plan. It does not accentuate the identity of each house, although Smithson admires Bath for being 'unmistakably a collection of separate houses'. It suppresses this in favour of visual syncopation, a partially randomised set of vertical fins, and horizontal continuity – the notion of a communal street deck. These 'streets in the air' have, surprisingly, all the faults which the Smithsons had recognised in other similar schemes. They are under-used; the collective entries are paltry and a few have been vandalised. Indeed, they are dark, smelly, dank passageways. Little sense of place, few collective facilities and fewer 'identifying elements', which the architects had reasonably said were needed in modern buildings.

36, 37 LAS VEGAS and EXETER CATHEDRAL CLOSE, two different kinds of social manifestations in which the architecture lends itself to direct symbolic expression. Regardless of our views of either social group, it has to be said that modern architects have disregarded this level of symbolic detail and particularity. Most cities contain ethnic diversity, but what large development incorporates the Chinese restaurant, the front of the local butcher? Architects have been too removed from this level of detail, and will be until they are retrained as anthropologists or journalists to understand social reality.

The Smithsons claim they have provided a sense of place.

> On the garden side the building is unified. It is an urban place, a part of the definition of a city, provided it does not become a repetitive pattern which organizes an homogeneous space.[5]

Indeed the space isn't homogeneous, it has kinks and an artificial mound near the centre. But these deviations from the norm and the subtle cues of visual separation are hardly strong enough to override the repetitive pattern and homogeneous material. These signify more strongly 'council housing', 'anonymity', 'the authorities didn't have enough money to use wood, stucco, etc.' – in short, they signify 'social deprivation'. The Smithsons' laudable intentions of providing a community building on the scale of the Bath Crescent and offering the same degree of individual expression and identity in an architectural language understood by all – these positive aims are denied by the built form.

Such contradictions between statement and result have reached impressive proportions in modern architecture, and one can now speak of a 'credibility gap' that parallels the loss of trust in politicians. The root causes of this are, I believe, based on the nature of architecture as a language. It is *radically schizophrenic* by necessity, partly rooted in tradition, in the past – indeed in everyone's childhood experience of crawling around on flat floors and perceiving such normal architectural elements as vertical doors. And it is partly rooted in a fast-changing society, with its new functional tasks, new materials, new technologies and ideologies. On the one hand, architecture is as slow-changing as spoken language (we can still understand Renaissance English); and, on the other, as fast-changing and esoteric as modern art and science.

Put another way, we learn from the beginning the cultural signs which make any urban place particular to a social group, an economic class and real, historical people; whereas modern architects spend their time unlearning all these particular signs in an attempt to design for universal man, or Mythic Modern Man. This

EXETER CATHEDRAL CLOSE

3-M monster of course doesn't exist, except as a historical fiction – the creation of modern novelists, sociologists and idealistic planners. Mr Triple-M is no doubt a logical necessity for architects and others who want to generalise a statistical average. Tom Wolfe has criticised novelists for writing about such non-existing creatures, and the same points could be scored against architects.[6] They try to provide modern man with a mythic consciousness, with consistent patterns reminiscent of tribal societies, refined in their purity, full of tasteful 'unity in variety', and other such geometric harmonies; when in fact modern man doesn't exist, and what he would want if he did perchance exist would be realistic social signs. Signs of status, history, commerce, comfort, ethnic domain, signs of being neighbourly, (though also a bit better off than the Joneses). Modern architects aren't trained in these codes, they don't know how to get close to this reality, and so they go on providing a mythic integration of community, (often now a projection of middle-class values).

Too bad: society can go on without architects, person-alise its housing estates or blow them up, or hire interior decorators. It doesn't matter (except in Russia); there are always other realistic professions who are ready to move in.

In any case, before we finish with this modern archi-tecture-bashing (a form of sadism which is getting far too easy), we should mention one dilemma architects face, (which isn't entirely of their own making), because it has an effect on the language they use.

Univalent content

Let us now examine the major commissions, the most prevalent building types which have engaged the skill of architects in this century. A certain disinterest is needed here, because the truths are hard and the solutions not forthcoming. Many will deny or gloss over the social realities behind architecture because they are so trivial and depressing and of no one's desire, no one's fault. The major mistake architects made in this century, on this score, is perhaps to have been born at all.

36, 37

Let us look anyway at the major monuments of modern architecture and the social tasks for which they were built. Here we will find a strange but unnoticed deflection of the modern architect's *role as a social utopian*, for we will see that he has actually built for the reigning powers of an established, commercial society; and this surreptitious liaison has taken its toll, as illicit love affairs will. The modern movement of architecture, conceived in the 1850s as a call to morality, and in the 1920s (in its Heroic Period) as a call to social transformation, found itself unwittingly compromised, first by practice and then by acceptance.[7] These architects wished to give up their subservient role as 'tailors' to society and what they regarded as 'a corrupt ruling taste', and become instead 'doctors', leaders, prophets, or at least midwives, to a new social order. But for what order did they build?

1 **Monopolies and big business.** Some of the accepted classics of modern architecture were built for clients who today are multinational corporations. Peter Behrens' Berlin Turbine Factory was for the General Electric of its day, AEG. This building of 1909 is often considered the first great work of European modern architecture because of its pure volumetric expression, its clear clean use of glass and steel, almost the curtain wall, and its refinement of utilitarian products — the beginning of industrial design. Further landmarks of architecture, those that modified the language slightly, were Frank Lloyd Wright's curvilinear poetry of pyrex tubing and streamlined brick, built for a large wax company; Gordon Bunshaft's classic solution for the office tower, two pure slabs set at right angles, one on top of the other, erected for the multinational based on soap; Mies van der Rohe's dark, Rolls-Royce solution to the curtain wall built for the Seagram's Whiskey giant; Eero Saarinen's walk-through bird-of-prey built for TWA; and numerous refinements of the curtain wall built by the large offices, such as Skidmore, Owings and Merrill, for soft drink companies, tobacco chains, international banks and oil companies. How should one express the power and concentration of capital, the mercantile function, the exploitation of markets? These building tasks would be the monuments of our time, because they bring in the extra money for architecture; and yet their potential role as social paragons is without credibility.

38 PETER BEHRENS, *AEG Factory*, Berlin, 1909. Often regarded as one of the first great modern buildings, the fountainhead too of industrial design, this work set the factory as the major metaphor for subsequent building. Here the marriage was made between big business, 'good design', and the functional style. This union was eagerly sought for at the time by the German *Werkbund,* and it bore multi-national fruit sixty years later. (Bauhaus Archive).

39 FRANK LLOYD WRIGHT, *Johnson Wax Building*, Racine, Wisconsin, 1938. Columns taper downwards and are supported on brass shoes. Everything takes up the curve theme in this 'total work of art'. The idea of a unified corporate image became standard by the fifties for such multinationals as the CBS, IBM, Olivetti, etc. (US Information Service).

Opposite
40 GORDON BUNSHAFT and SOM, *Lever Brothers Building*, New York City, 1951–2. The first convincing use of the light curtain wall. Spandrels and glass alternate in horizontal bands which are then covered by a neutral mesh of mullions. By the sixties, many multi-nationals on Park Avenue had similar corporate boxes.

41 JOHN KIBBLE, *Glasgow Botanic Garden,* 1873. Recreated from a former building as 'the Crystal Art Palace', this glasshouse recalls Indian architecture and onion domes. The large squashed dome at the back is 146ft across, and had at its centre a lily pond in which an orchestra played : the ceiling opened and closed for diminuendo and crescendo. (Easter Young).

2 International exhibitions, World Fairs.

Another geneology of modern architecture is traced from the Crystal Palace of 1851 to the Theme Pavilion at Osaka 1970. This line of descent has a series of technical triumphs to its credit, resulting in the new language of lattice structures, the open girders of Eiffel, the pin-jointed parabolas of industrial sheds, the translucent and geometric domes of Buckminster Fuller, and the soaring tents of Frei Otto (these tents always soar in architectural criticism). Indeed these triumphs did a great deal to aestheticise the experience of architecture : historians and critics skipped lightly over the content of the structures, their propagandist role ; and focused instead on their spatial and optical qualities. The mass media followed suit. Overlooked was the blatant nationalism and ersatz ambience which constituted ninety per cent of the World Fairs. Why ? Because this ignored content was so obviously hedonistic and lacking in subtlety, and because there was no great understanding of how this blatant content works in mass culture, nor how it is occasionally humorous, creative and provocative.

Opposite above
42 KENZO TANGE, *Theme Pavilion, EXPO 70,* Osaka, 1970. A megastructure carrying various services was finally built after being contemplated by the avant-garde for ten years. World Fairs often allow such grandiose and creative ideas to be realised, and have therefore played an important role in the evolution of modern architecture. (Masao Arai).

Opposite below
43 The CAMBODIAN PAVILION, Osaka, 1970. Designed with the advice of Prince Norodom Sihanouk, this typically nationalist pavilion echoes Khmer architecture and Angkor Vat. Most World's Fair architecture has an air of pastiche about it which could offend convinced nationalists, but it conforms to mass standards of propriety. This manifestation is overlooked by serious critics and remains undiscussed. (Japan Information Service).

44 PATRICK HODGKINSON, *Foundling Estate,* London, 1973. Long lines of housing with greenhouse living-rooms are stacked on the diagonal. The grand public entrance, the largest of its kind in Great Britain, looks as if it leads to a ceremonial space, at least a stadium, but it actually culminates in an empty plaza. The Futurist styling and semantic confusion are again a consequence of the modern movement's rejection of rhetoric and a theory of communication.

Below
45 RICHARD ROGERS and RENZO PIANO, *Pompidou Centre,* Paris, 1977. Gigantic trusses manufactured by Krupp and brought through Paris streets early in the morning, hold up this spiky cultural centre. The technological image is carried through with conviction, especially on the services which are painted in strong primary colours. By sinking the building and breaking up its facade, the scale is sympathetic with the traditional Paris street pattern. (Bernard Vincent).

3 **Factories and engineering feats.** From Walter Gropius' Fagus Factory, 1911, to Le Corbusier's 'home as a machine for living in', 1922, we have the birth and establishment of the major metaphor for modern architecture: the factory. Housing was conceived in this image, and the Nazis were not altogether wrong in attacking the first international manifesto of this metaphor, the *Weissenhof Siedlungen*, 1927, for its inappropriateness. Why should houses adopt the imagery of the mass production line and the white purity of the hospital?

44

46 More recent mass housing in England, for instance that in London, or Milton Keynes, has followed this pervasive twentieth-century metaphor. That no one asked to live in a factory did not occur to the doctor-modern-architect, because he was out to cure the disease of modern cities, no matter how distasteful the medicine. Indeed, better if it tasted like castor oil and caused convulsions, because then the transformation of bourgeois society was more likely to be complete, the patient would reform his petty acquisitive drives and become a good collectivised citizen.

Such metaphors for housing have been rejected almost everywhere they've been applied, (exceptions occur in Germany and Switzerland), but they have taken hold in appropriate areas: stadia, sports grounds, aircraft hangars,

5, 47 and all the large-span structures traditionally associated with engineering. Here the poetry of process is exhilarating

46 JEREMY DIXON, CHRIS CROSS and ED JONES, *'Netherfield' Milton Keynes Housing*, 1974. Another long line, now accentuated by structural fins and a flat roof plane, is the apotheosis of the assembly-line metaphor applied to housing. (John Donat).

47 KENZO TANGE, *National Gymnasia for the Olympic Games*, Tokyo, 1964. Two buildings in subtle counterpoint are placed on a podium. The concrete masts, which hold the hyperbolic curves, end in the typical Japanese 'slant' which has become something of a cliché. The gentle curves and structural expression are also traditional signs.

without being wildly inappropriate or surreal, and we can claim the single, unmitigated triumph of modern architecture on the level of content.

4 Consumer temples and churches of distraction.
Someone from an alien culture would be amazed to see, if he took a quick helicopter trip over any of our sprawling cities, that urban man worshipped at institutions devoted to commercial gods. Modern architects haven't altogether mastered this territory of Disneyland and ride-through parks, of Kings Road and Sunset Strip, but they are beginning to try, and we can already count the triumphs. The exquisite technological jewels of Hans Hollein, the 48-5 boutiques and candle shops, and high-gloss mausolea given over to selling religious relics for the wedding finger. So much design talent and mystery expended on such small shops would convince an outsider that he had at last stumbled on the true faith of this civilisation. And when he came to see the same medals worshipped in the

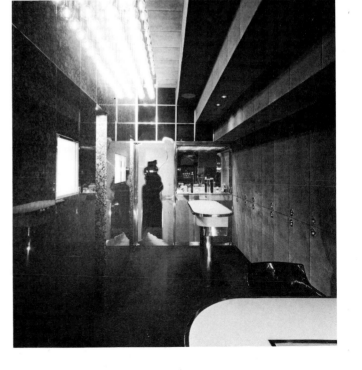

48, 49 HANS HOLLEIN, *Jewellery Shop*, Vienna, 1975. Hollein uses voluptuous, shiny marble to set off the polished mechanical equipment. The contrast of circle and fissure, of skin-like marble and the glistening gold lips folding over each other, is explicitly ironic and sexual. Tight space is ingeniously cut up to loosen the customer's libido even further. Perhaps only a Viennese could have brought off this mixture of commerce and sensuality. (Jerzy Surwillo).

50 HANS HOLLEIN, *Jewellery Shop*, Vienna, 1975.

51, 52 JOHN PORTMAN, *Bonaventure Hotel*, model, Los Angeles, 1976. Portman has revived the nineteenth-century tradition of the grand hotel — at least the cost part of this tradition — with his lavish Regency Hyatts in several American cities. He gives the exteriors an absolute geometric image, parts of which in mirrorplate reflect like overblown jewels. The planning is reminiscent of the megalomaniacal schemes of Boullée.

large hotels, constructed in the theological material of mirrorplate, his interpretation would be confirmed. The culture idolises tinsel, personal adornment, private jewellery. The more adept modern architects become at embellishing buildings (and of course they are working at a distinct disadvantage, having previously equated 'ornament' and 'crime'), the more the anomaly appears. A jewel is a jewel, is not a fitting object for great architecture. The banality of content will not go away.

Architecture obviously reflects what a society holds important, what it values both spiritually and in terms of cash. In the pre-industrial past the major areas for expression were the temple, the church, the palace, agora, meeting house, country house and city hall; while in the present, extra money is spent on hotels, restaurants and all those commercial building types I have mentioned. Public housing and buildings expressing the local community or the public realm receive the cutbacks. Buildings representing consumer values generate the investment. As Galbraith says of American capitalism, it results in private wealth and public squalor.

Several modern architects, in a desperate attempt to cheer themselves up, have decided that since this is an inevitable situation, it must also have its good points. Commercial tasks are more democratic than the previous aristocratic and religious ones; 'Main Street is almost all right' according to Robert Venturi.

When these commercial design tasks first emerged into consciousness, about the turn of this century, they were celebrated by the Futurist, Sant' Elia, with a glee and moralising tone that were later to become common. He contrasted the new building tasks, given over to commerce and energy, with the previous ones devoted to worship — the nineteenth-century dynamo versus the thirteenth-century Virgin.

The formidable antithesis between the modern world and the old is determined by all those things that formerly did not exist . . . we have lost our predilection for the monumental, the heavy, the static, and we have enriched our sensibility with a *taste for the light, the practical, the ephemeral and the swift*. We no longer feel ourselves to be the men of the cathedrals, the palaces and the tribunes. We are the men of the great

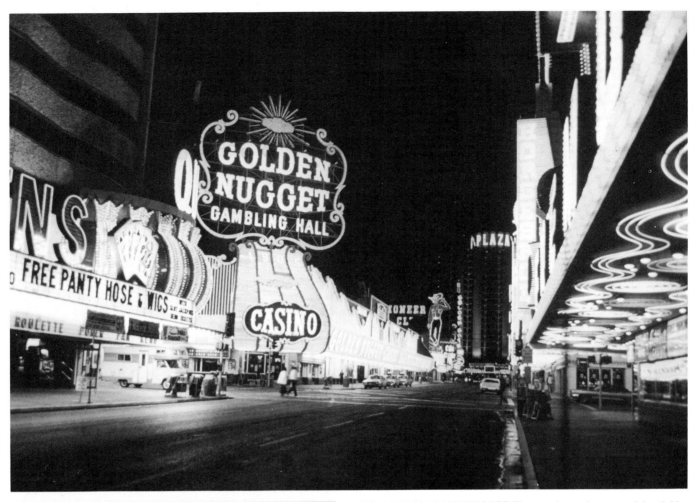

53 LAS VEGAS LIGHTSCAPE. The secular and commercial activities celebrated by the Futurists are realised here with a technological artistry they would have relished, but a social content on which they would have choked.

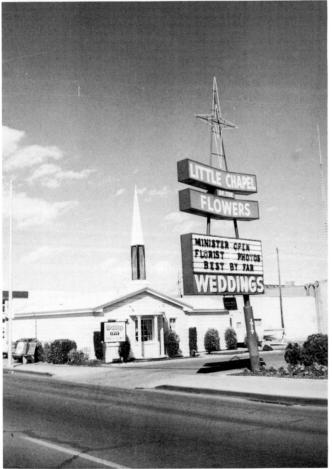

54 LITTLE CHAPEL of the FLOWERS, Las Vegas, 1960. Drive-in marriage and divorce, your Olde New England clapboard church advertised in neon, with totally automated services – a combination which is far too new and old at the same time, but one which appeals to vast numbers in a consumer society.

hotels, the railway stations, the immense streets, colossal ports, covered markets, luminous arcades, straight roads and beneficial demolitions. [8]

In short, these embrace the social activities of a middle-class tourist wandering from railway station to hotel along wide super-highways dotted with bulldozed sites and lit by sparkling neon signs. With slight modifications, Sant'

53 Elia could be describing the glitter of Las Vegas, or less fashionably, let us say, the main street of Warsaw. Whatever the country, whatever the economic system, such secular building tasks are the important ones today, and so much modern art and architecture tries to celebrate this fact. 'The heroism of everyday life', that notion shared by Picasso, Léger and Le Corbusier in the twenties, was a philosophy which tried to place banal objects on a pedestal formerly reserved for special symbols of veneration. The fountain pen, the filing cabinet, the steel girder and the typewriter were the new icons. Mayakovsky and the Russian Constructivists took art into the streets and even performed one grand symphony of sirens and steam whistles, while waving coloured flags on top of factory roofs. The hope of these artists and architects was to reform society on a new class and functional basis: substitute power stations for cathedrals, technocrats for aristocrats. A new, heroic, democratic society would emerge, led by a powerful race of pagan supermen, the avant-garde, the technicians and captains of industry, the enlightened scientists and teams of experts. What a dream!

Indeed, the managerial revolution did occur, and socialist revolutions happened in a few countries; but the dream was taken over by Madison Avenue (and its equivalents), and the 'heroic object of everyday use' became the 'new, revolutionary detergent'. Societies kept on worshipping at their old altars, with diminishing faith, and tried to incorporate the new values at the same time. The result? Ersatz culture, a caricature of the past and 54 future at once, a surreal fantasy dreamed up neither by the avant-garde, nor the traditionalists, and abhorrent to both of them.

With the triumph of consumer society in the West and bureaucratic State Capitalism in the East, our unfortunate modern architect was left without much uplifting social content to symbolise. If architecture has to concentrate its efforts on symbolising a way of life and the public realm, then it's in a bit of a fix when these things lose their credibility. There's nothing much the architect can do about this except protest as a citizen, and design dissenting buildings that express the complex situation. He can communicate the values which are missing and ironically criticise the ones he dislikes. But to do that he must make use of the language of the local culture, otherwise his message falls on deaf ears, or is distorted to fit this local language.

55 ADOLF LOOS, *Chicago Tribune Column.*

PART TWO
The Modes of Architectural Communication

Monsieur Jourdain, Molière's *Bourgeois Gentilhomme*, was rather surprised to discover that he had been speaking prose for forty years – 'without knowing anything about it'. Modern architects might suffer a similar shock, or doubt that they've been speaking anything as elevated as prose. To look at the environment is to agree with their doubt. We see a babble of tongues, a free-for-all of personal idiolects, not the classical language of the Doric, Ionic and Corinthian Orders. Where there once were rules of architectural grammar, we now have a mutual diatribe between speculative builders; where there once was a gentle discourse between the Houses of Parliament and Westminster Abbey, there is now across the Thames, the Shell Building shouting at the Hayward Gallery, which grunts back at a stammering and giggling Festival Hall. It's all confusion and strife, and yet this invective is still language even if it's not very comprehensible or persuading. There *are* various analogies architecture shares with language and if we use the terms loosely, we can speak of architectural 'words', 'phrases', 'syntax', and 'semantics'. I will discuss several of these analogies in turn, showing how they can be more consciously used as communicational means, starting with the mode most commonly disregarded in modern architecture.

Below
56 SAN FRANCISCO CITYSCAPE, 1973. With various skyscrapers, including a trussed rectangle and the triangular building, known affectionately as 'Pereiras' Prick' (he designed the Transamerican Corporation).

Below
57 The SOUTH BANK, London, 1976. With large chunks devoted to different functions: *left to right:* The Queen Elizabeth Hall, Royal Festival Hall and Shell Tower carry on their distinctive form of garbled conversation. Each chunk sends out a single, if muted, message that it is an 'important' monument of some unspecified kind.

Metaphor

People invariably see one building in terms of another, or in terms of a similar object; in short as a metaphor. The more unfamiliar a modern building is, the more they will compare it metaphorically to what they know. This matching of one experience to another is a property of all thought, particularly that which is creative. Thus when pre-cast concrete grills were first used on buildings in the late fifties, they were seen as 'cheesegraters', 'beehives', 'chain-link fences'; while ten years later when they became the norm in a certain building type, they were seen in functional terms: 'this looks like a parking garage'. From metaphor to cliché, from neologism through constant usage to architectural **sign**, this is the continual route travelled by new and successful forms and technics.

Typical negative metaphors used by the public and by critics such as Lewis Mumford to condemn modern architecture were 'cardboard box', 'shoe-box', 'egg-crate', 'filing cabinet', 'grid-paper'. These comparisons were sought not only for their pejorative, mechanistic overtones,

but also because they were strongly **coded** in a culture which had become sensitised to the spectre of 1984. This obvious point has some curious implications, as we shall see.

One implication became apparent when I was visiting Japan and the architect Kisho Kurokawa. We went to see his new apartment tower in Tokyo, made from stacked shipping containers, which had a most unusual overall shape. They looked like stacked sugar cubes, or even more, like superimposed washing machines, because the white cubes all had round windows in their centres. When I said this metaphor had unfortunate overtones for living, Kurokawa evinced suprise. 'They aren't washing machines, they're bird cages. You see in Japan we build concrete-box bird nests with round holes and place them in the trees. I've built these bird nests for itinerant businessmen who visit Tokyo, for bachelors who fly in every so often with their birds.' A witty answer, perhaps made up on the spot, but one which underscored very nicely a difference in our visual codes.

60 A well-known visual illusion brings this out even more: the famous 'duck-rabbit figure', which will be seen first one way then the other. Since we all have well learned visual codes for *both* animals, and even probably now a code for the hybrid monster with two heads, we can see it three ways. One view may predominate, according to either the strength of the code or according to the direction from which we see the figure at first. To get further readings ('bellows' or 'keyhole' etc.) is harder because these codes are less strong for this figure, they map less well than the primary ones – at least in our culture. The general point then is *that code restrictions based on learning and culture guide a reading, and that there are multiple codes, some of which may be in conflict across subcultures.* In very general terms there are two large subcultures: one with the modern code based on the training and ideology of modern architects, and another with the traditional code based on everyone's experience of normalised architectural elements. As I mentioned, (*above* page 24), there are very basic reasons why these codes may be at odds and architecture may be radically schizophrenic, both in its creation and interpretation. Since some buildings often incorporate various codes, they can be seen as mixed metaphors, and with opposing meanings: e.g. the 'harmonious, well-proportioned pure volume' of the modern architect becomes the 'shoe-box' or 'filing cabinet' to the public.

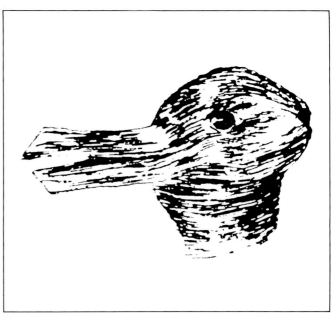

60 The DUCK-RABBIT ILLUSION, read from left to right by duck hunters and from right to left by frequenters of the Playboy Club. Since this illusion is so well known we can now see it as a new animal with two heads. But note: you can only read it one way at a time *depending on the code you choose to adopt.* (E. H. Gombrich, *Art and Illusion*).

61 JORN UTZON, *Sydney Opera House,* Australia, 1957–74. A mixed metaphor: the shells have symbolised flowers unfolding, sailboats in the harbour, fish swallowing each other and now, because of the local code, high cost. As with the Eiffel Tower, ambiguous meanings have finally transcended all possible functional considerations and the building has become simply a national symbol. This rare class of sign, like a Rorschach test, provokes response which focuses interest on the responder, not the sign. It could be called the 'enigmatic sign', because, like the ocean, it happily receives projected meanings from everyone. (New South Wales Government Office, London).

61 One modern building, the Sydney Opera House, has provoked a superabundance of metaphorical responses, both in the popular and professional press. The reasons are, again, that the forms are both unfamiliar to architecture and reminiscent of other visual objects. Most of the metaphors are organic: thus the architect, Jorn Utzon, showed how the shells of the building related to the surface of a sphere (like 'orange segments') and the wing of a bird in flight. They also relate, obviously, to white sea shells, and it is this metaphor, plus the comparison to the white sails bobbing around in Sydney Harbour, that have become journalistic clichés. This raises another obvious point with unexpected implications: the interpretation of architectural metaphor is more elastic and dependent on *local* codes than the interpretation of metaphor in spoken or written language.

Some critics have pointed out that the superimposed shells resemble the growth of a flower over time – the unfolding of petals; while architectural students of Aus-

62 tralia caricatured this same aspect as 'turtles making love'. From several points of view the violent aspect of broken and smashed up shapes is apparent – 'a traffic accident with no survivors'; while again these same views elicit possible organic metaphors – 'fish swallowing each other'. Reinforcing this interpretation are the shiny, scaly elements of the tiled surface which are apparent up close. But the most extraordinary metaphor, and the one which

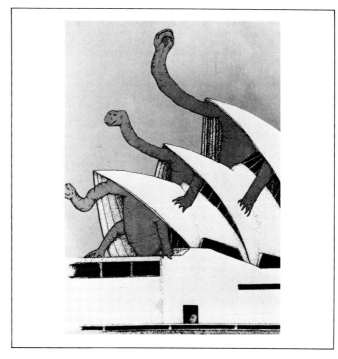

62 CARTOON presented by architectural students when Queen Elizabeth officially opened the building (from *Architecture in Australia*).

63 SYDNEY OPERA HOUSE, view of shells soaring and crashing, again an interesting ambiguity to be set along with the other mixed metaphors. Note the way the building glistens and takes on the cloud formations. (Australian Information Service).

Australians apply with a certain bemused affection, is 'scrum of nuns'. All those shells leaning over, confronting each other in two main directions, resemble the head-dresses and cowls of two opposed monastic orders, and the wildly unlikely idea that this could be a scrimmage of mother superiors dominates the possibilities. 'Wit' has been defined as 'the unlikely copulation of ideas together', and the more unlikely *but* successful the union, the more it will strike the viewer and stay in his mind. A witty building is one which permits us to make extraordinary but convincing associations.

The question obviously arises of how appropriate these metaphors are to the building's function and its symbolic role. Concentrating on this aspect and momentarily disregarding other things such as cost (the Australians spent something like twenty times the original estimate for their mixed metaphor) we might come to the following conclusion. On the one hand the organic metaphors are very appropriate to a cultural centre: images which suggest growth are particularly apt for meanings of creativity. The building flies, sails, splashes, curves up and unfolds like an animated vegetable. Fine. Perhaps if the building were renamed The Australian Cultural Centre (not the Sydney Opera House) and justified as a symbol of Australia's liberation from Anglo-Saxon dependence, (the overriding influence of Britain and America), then its interpretation might be clearer. We could then see these extraordinary metaphors in their most positive light, as symbols of Australia's break with colonial conformity and provinciality.

But doubts arise. We know the building was designed by a European (not an Australian) as an *opera* house – and one that works neither economically nor functionally in the manner it was conceived. Since such knowledge is an integral part of the code with which we interpret the building, our judgement cannot avoid being contaminated by this knowledge. It's rather like looking at the duck-rabbit figure: our perception is bent and shaped by codes based on previous experience. It is virtually impossible to perceive the building without knowing about the notorious 'Sydney Opera House Case', the firing of the architect, the cost, and so forth. So these local, specific meanings also become symbolised in the 'extravagant' shells.

Several modernists criticised the Opera House for other reasons: as a piece of literal communication the building tells you little and dissimulates much. You can't pick out the various theatres and restaurants and exhibition halls beneath the shells, which is why it has been so annoying to certain architects brought up in the tradition of expressive functionalism. They expect to see each function given a clear and separate volume, which ideally speaking, is an outline of the function – such as the auditorium. They would have designed the building as a series of boxy fly towers and wedge shapes (the conventionalised 'word' for auditorium in modern architecture). The building violates this code, as classical architecture

64 KONSTANTIN MELNIKOV, *Russakov Club,* Moscow, 1928. The wedge shape plus rectangular flytower became established as the 'word' for auditorium in the language of modern architecture because of this building. The shapes follow, more or less, the volumes needed for the functions.

often did, by obscuring actual functions behind overall patterns. The debate then becomes whether such obscurantism is justified by the wit and appropriateness of the organic metaphor. I think it is, but others would deny this.

Perhaps one of them would be Robert Venturi, who also starts from the position that architecture should be looked at as communication, but comes to different conclusions from mine. He contends that buildings should look like 'decorated sheds, not ducks'. The decorated shed is a simple enclosure with signs attached like a billboard, or the application of conventional ornament, such as a pediment symbolising entry; whereas a duck, for him, is a building in the shape of its function, (a bird-shaped building selling duck decoys), or a modern building where the construction, structure and volume become the decoration. Clearly the Sydney Opera House is a duck for Venturi, and he wishes to underplay this form of expression because he thinks it has been overdone by the modern movement. I would disagree with this historical judgement, and take even greater exception to the attitudes implied behind it. Venturi, like the typical modernist that he wishes to supplant, is adopting the tactic of exclusive inversion. He is cutting out a whole area of architectural communication, duck buildings, (technically speaking **iconic**

65
66

65 ROBERT VENTURI, *The Duck versus Decorated Shed*. Venturi would prefer more decorated sheds, because he contends, they communicate effectively, and modern architects have for too long only designed 'ducks'. The duck is, in semiotic terms, an *iconic* sign, because the signifier (form) has certain aspects in common with the signified (content). The decorated shed depends on learned meanings — writing or decoration — which are *symbolic* signs.

66 SECURITY MARINE BANK, Wisconsin, c. 1971. The *symbolic* shed, one part communication of status and security, the other part function. Commercial pressures today naturally dissociate signifier and signified in this way, although not usually so clearly. (Wayne Attoe).

signs), in order to make his preferred mode, decorated sheds (**symbolic** signs) that much more potent. Thus we are being asked, once more by a modernist, in the name of rationality, to follow an exclusive, simplistic path. Clearly we need all the modes of communication at our disposal, not one or two; and it's the modernist commitment to architectural street-fighting that leads to such oversimplification, not a balanced theory of signification.

In any case, the Sydney Opera House does pose some difficult problems as a duck, because of its lack of a shared, public symbolism — a point Venturi's extreme position brings out. While the organic metaphors are suitable analogues for a culture centre, they are not reinforced by conventional signs which spring from the Australian vernacular, and therefore they have an erratic signification. Rather, they emanate from the widespread formalist movement of modern architects, a movement which might be more appropriately termed surrealist. Like a Magritte painting — the apple which expands to fill a whole room — the meaning is striking but enigmatic and ultimately evasive. What precisely is Utzon trying to say, beyond the primitive and exciting? Why, besides creativity, all the sails, shells, flowers, fish and nuns? Clearly our emotions are being heightened as an end in themselves, and there is no exact goal towards which all these meanings converge. They float around in our mind to pick up connections where they will, like a luxuriant dream following overindulgence.

They do however prove a general point about communication: the more the metaphors, the greater the drama, and the more they are slightly suggestive, the greater the mystery. A mixed metaphor is strong, as every student of Shakespeare knows, but a suggested one is powerful. In architecture, to name a metaphor is often to kill it, like analysing jokes. When hot dog stands are in the

108 shape of hot dogs, then little work is left to the imagination, and all other metaphors are suppressed: they can't even suggest hamburgers. Yet even this kind of univalent metaphor, the Pop architecture of Los Angeles, has its imaginative and communicative side. For one thing, the customary scale and context are violently distorted, so the

67 ordinary object, for instance the doughnut, takes on a series of possible meanings not usually associated with this item of food. When it's blown up to thirty feet and built out of wood and sits on a small building, it becomes the Magritte object that has taken over the house from the occupants. Partly hostile and menacing, it is nevertheless a symbol of sugary breakfasts and *Gemütlichkeit*.

Secondly, an architecture made up from such signs communicates unambiguously to those moving fifty miles per hour through the city. In contrast with so much modern building, these iconic signs speak with exactitude and humour about their function. Their literalism, however infantile, articulates factual truths which Mies' work obscures, and there is a certain general pleasure (which doesn't escape children) in perceiving a sequence of them. Contrary to Venturi, we need more ducks; modern architects haven't propagated enough.

One who tried was Eero Saarinen. Immediately after he selected Utzon's Opera House as the winner of the competition, he returned to America and designed his own version of the curvilinear, shell building. The TWA ter-

69 minal in New York is an icon of a bird, and by extension, of aeroplane flight. In the details and merging of circulation lines, of passenger exits and crossways, it is a particularly clever working out of this metaphor. A

70 supporting strut is mapped to a bird's leg, the rain-spout becomes an ominous beak, an interior bridge covered in

71 blood-red carpet becomes, I suppose, the pulmonary artery. Here the imaginative meanings add up in an appropriate and calculated way, pointing towards a common metaphor of flight — the mutual interaction of these meanings produces a multivalent work of architecture.

67 HENRY J. GOODWIN, *Big Donut Drive-in*, Los Angeles, 1954. Originally there were ten of these giants, now there are, alas, three. The doughnuts sold are big.

68 DINOSAUR, Los Angeles, 1973. A curio shop which actually sells a few old bones, among other things. Los Angeles had a great deal of Pop architecture in the twenties and thirties, but most of it has been supplanted by the slick commercial symbols of chains, such as MacDonalds Hamburgers. (Environmental Communications).

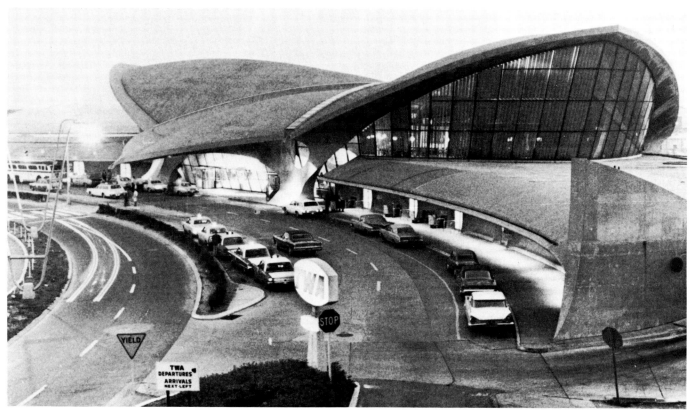

69 EERO SAARINEN, *TWA Building,* New York, 1962. Designed after Saarinen judged the Sydney Opera House competition. Here the concrete shells are clearly recognisable as a metaphor of flight, although there are other animals suggested. (TWA).

70 TWA BUILDING. The leg of the bird is at the same time a beautiful abstraction of structural forces.

71 TWA BUILDING. The red carpet swoops over the entry space, curve and counter-curve reinforce the feeling of continuous movement – all appropriate for a transportation building.

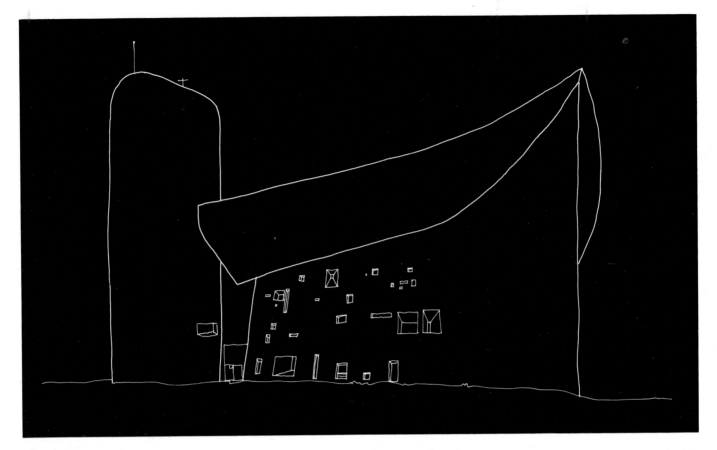

The most effective use of *suggested* metaphor that I can think of in modern architecture is Le Corbusier's chapel at Ronchamp which has been compared to all sorts of things, varying from the white houses of Mykonos to Swiss cheese. Part of its power is this suggestiveness – to mean many different things at once, to set the mind off on a wild goose chase where it actually catches the goose, among other animals. For instance a duck (once again this famous character of modern architecture) is vaguely suggested in the south elevation; but so also are a ship and, appropriately, praying hands. The visual codes, which here take in both elitist and popular meanings, are working mostly on an unconscious level, unlike the hot dog stand. We read the metaphors immediately without bothering to name or draw them (as done here), and clearly the skill of the artist is dependent on his ability to call up our rich storehouse of visual images without our being aware of his intention. Perhaps it is also a somewhat unconscious process for him. Le Corbusier only admitted to two metaphors, both of which are esoteric: the 'visual acoustics' of the curving walls which shape the four horizons as if they were 'sounds', (responding in antiphony), and the 'crab shell' form of the roof. But the building has many more metaphors than this, so many that it is overcoded, saturated with possible interpretations. This explains why critics such as Pevsner and Stirling have found the building so upsetting, and others have found it so enigmatic. It seems to suggest precise ritualistic meanings, it looks like the temple of some very complicated sect which reached a high degree of metaphysical sophistication; whereas we *know* it is simply a pilgrimage chapel created by someone who believed in a natural religion, a pantheism.

Put another way, Ronchamp creates the fascination that the discovery of a new archaic language does; we stumble upon this Rosetta stone, this fragment of a lost civilisation,

72, 73 LE CORBUSIER, *Ronchamp Chapel,* France, 1955. View from the south-east. The building is over-coded with visual metaphors, and none of them is very explicit, so that the building seems always about to tell us something which we just can't place. The effect can be compared to having a word on the tip of your tongue which you can't quite remember. But the ambiguity can be dramatic, not frustrating – you search your memory for the possible clues.

and every time we decode its surface we come up with coherent meanings we know do not refer to any precise social practice – as they appear to do. Le Corbusier has so overcoded his building with metaphor, and so precisely related part to part, that the meanings seem as if they had been fixed by countless generations engaged in ritual: something as rich as the delicate patterns of Islam, the exact iconology of Shinto, is suggested. How frustrating, how enjoyable it is to experience this game of signification, which we know rests mostly on imaginative brilliance.

48

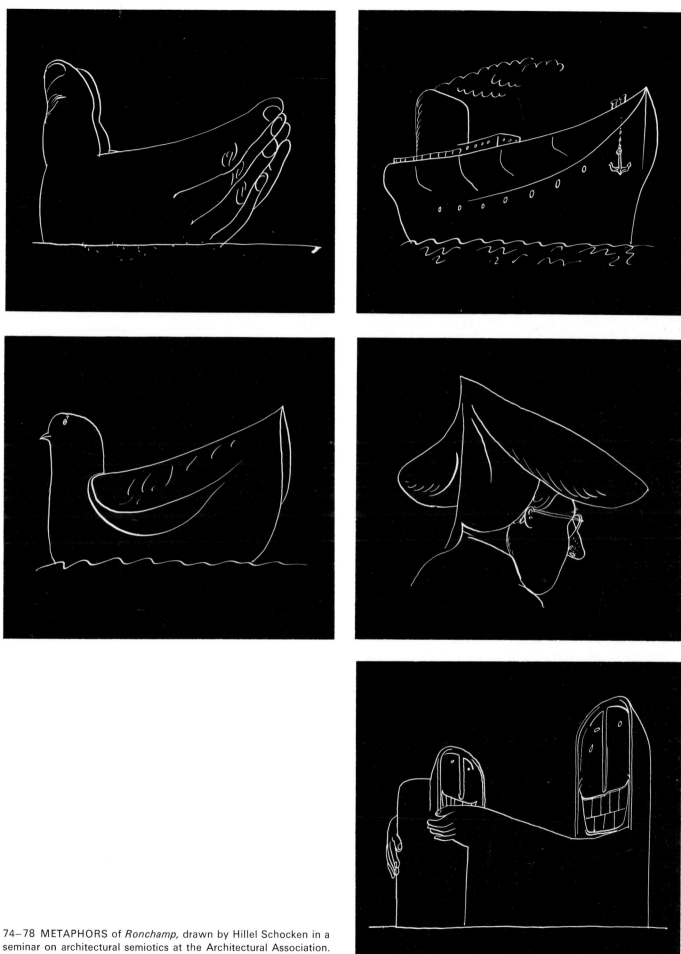

74—78 METAPHORS of *Ronchamp,* drawn by Hillel Schocken in a seminar on architectural semiotics at the Architectural Association. The mapping is amazingly literal when compared to the actual views.

79 CESAR PELLI, *Pacific Design Center,* Los Angeles, 1976. A long, high building which looks like an extruded moulding, among other things, because its section is projected throughout the building and on the end elevations. This metaphor is appropriate to its function, since the building displays the mouldings of interior designers (among other products). Its blue exterior, in translucent, transparent and reflective glass, gives it a startling presence in Los Angeles; and because of its size, it is known as 'The Blue Whale'. (Marvin Rand).

Opposite

80 PDC metaphors seen in a seminar on architectural semiotics, UCLA, 1976, drawn by Kamran. The metaphors were voted on by the class and placed in the following order of plausibility: **1** aircraft hangar, **2** extrusion or architectural moulding, **3** station or terminal building, **4** model of a building, **5** warehouse, **6** blue ice-berg, **7** prison, **8** a child's building-blocks or puzzle. The fact that so many metaphors turned out to be actual building types (e.g. 'station or terminal') shows that the PDC recalls other architecture quite strongly.

Another modern building which crystallises a series of metaphors, because of its unusual shape, is Cesar Pelli's Pacific Design Center in Los Angeles – known locally as 'the Blue Whale'. Opposed to Ronchamp and TWA, it makes use of rectilinear forms and a curtain wall of three different types of glass, but these familiar elements nonetheless call up unfamiliar associations because of their peculiar treatment: 'iceberg', 'cash register', 'aircraft hangar', and most appropriately 'extruded architectural moulding', (it's a centre for interior decorators and designers).

These metaphors can be mapped quite literally in terms of outline shape and section; not so the 'Blue Whale' image which relates only in terms of colour and mass. And yet this is the favoured nickname. Why? Because there happens to be a local restaurant whose doorway is a large blue whale's mouth, and the building is recognised as a leviathan in its small-scaled neighbourhood swallowing up all the little fish, (in this case the diminutive decorators shops). In other words, two local pertinent codes, the large scale and the connection with the local restaurant, take precedence over the more plausible metaphors of the building, the aircraft hangar or moulding – a good example of the way architecture is even more at the mercy of the perceiver than, say, poetry.

Architecture as a language is much more malleable than the spoken language, and subject to the transformations of short-lived codes. While a building may stand 300 years, the way people regard and use it may change every ten years. It would be perverse to rewrite Shakespearean sonnets, change love poetry to hate letters, read comedy as tragedy; but it is perfectly acceptable to hang washing on decorative balustrades, convert a church into a concert hall, and use a building every day while never looking at it, (actually the norm). Architecture is often experienced inattentively or with the greatest prejudice of mood and will – exactly opposite to the way one is supposed to experience a symphony or work of art.[12] One implication of this for architecture is that, among other things, the architect must overcode his buildings, using a redundancy of popular signs and metaphors, if his work is to communicate as intended and survive the transformation of fast-changing codes.

Surprisingly, many modern architects deny this most potent metaphorical level of meaning. They find it non-functional and personal, literary and vague, certainly not something they can consciously control and use appropriately. Instead they concentrate on the supposedly rational aspects of design – the cost and function, as they narrowly define them. The result is that their inadvertent metaphors take metaphorical revenge and kick them in the behind: their buildings end up looking like metaphors of

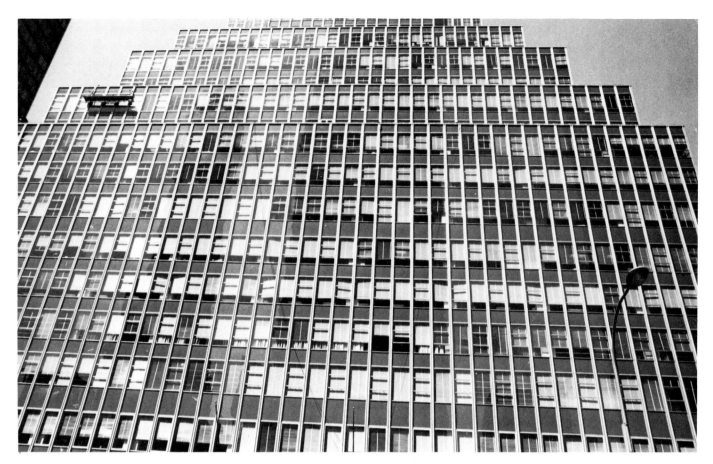

81 MANUFACTURERS HANOVER TRUST, New York, 1970. This kind of building on Park Avenue and elsewhere is often satirised by cartoonists such as Steinburg and Kovarsky, who will represent it as grid paper, bank account statement, or any number of economic graphs which rise and fall.

81 function and economics, and are condemned as such. The situation is bound to change, however, as both social research and architectural semiotics demonstrate the interpersonal, shared response to metaphor. This is much more predictable and controllable than architects have thought; and since metaphor plays a predominant role in the public's acceptance or rejection of buildings, one can bet that architects will see the point, if only for their own prosperity. Metaphor, seen through conventional visual codes, differs from group to group; but it can be coherently, if not precisely, delineated for all these groups in a society.

Words
Underlying much of what I have been saying so far is the notion of cliché – the fact that the architectural language, like the spoken one, must use known units of meaning. To make the linguistic analogy complete, we could call these units architectural 'words'. There are dictionaries of architecture which define the meanings of these words: doors, windows, columns, partitions, cantilevers, and so forth. Obviously these repeated elements are a necessity of architectural practice. The building industry standardises countless products, (there are over 400 building systems in Britain), and the architectural office repeats its favourite details.

As in language, yesterday's creative metaphor becomes today's tired usage, a conventional word. I have mentioned that the wedge shape became a sign of auditoria, and that concrete grills – the cheesegrater metaphor –

became, largely, the sign of a parking garage ('office' is the secondary usage). Yet there is a crucial difference between the 'words' of architecture and of speech. Consider the case of the column. A column on a building is one 82 thing, the Nelson Column in Trafalgar Square another, the 83 column smoke-stack at Battersea Power Station in 84 London a third, and Adolf Loos' entry for the Chicago 85 Tribune Column a fourth. If the column is a 'word', then the word has become a phrase, a sentence and finally a 86 whole novel. Clearly architectural words are more elastic and polymorphous than those of spoken or written language, and are more based on their physical context and the code of the viewer for their specific sense. To determine what 'Nelson's Column' means you have to analyse the social-physical context, ('Trafalgar Square as a centre for political rallies'), the semantic overtones of Nelson, ('naval victories,' 'historical figure' etc.), the syntactic markers, ('standing alone', 'surrounded by open space and fountains'), and the historical connotations of column, ('use on temples', 'Three Orders', 'phallic symbol' etc.). Such an analysis is beyond the scope of this book, but an initial attempt has been made for analysing the column in general, which shows how fruitful this can be.[11] We can make a componential analysis of architectural elements and find out which are, for any culture, distinctive units.

Modern architects have not always faced up to the implications of clichés, or traditional words. They have, by and large, tried to avoid the re-use of **symbolic signs** (the technical term for meaning set by conventional usage)

82–86 The COLUMN as a 'WORD', seen in different contexts, changes its meaning. At ST MARTIN-IN-THE-FIELD, London, 1726, it is seen on a portico with other columns of the same order – clearly signifying 'colonnade', 'entrance', 'public building' as well as historical associations. The NELSON COLUMN, Trafalgar Square, 1860, shifts the semantic overtones towards commemoration, 'victory', 'politics'. 'standing alone' etc. The COLUMN-SMOKE-STACKS at BATTERSEA POWER STATION, London, 1929–55, have entirely different associations, because of their syntactic properties. They are placed above a massive base on four corners (incidentally this is now *the* sign of power station), and so the building looks mildly like an overturned table. Smoke belches out the top – which has no capital or entablature – so the 'fluted columns have been violated'. Adolf Loos' CHICAGO TRIBUNE COLUMN, a competition entry for a newspaper, was a double pun on the word column ('newspaper column', 'tribune', the name of the newspaper). Loos felt that the Doric Order was a most basic statement of architectural order and therefore fitting for a monument. Finally, the KENTON COUNTY WATER TOWER, Ohio, 1955, again shows the polyvalent aspect of this vertical shape, how it can be used on elevator shafts, chimneys, rocket launchers and oil derricks. Because of the column's positive associations with antiquity, it is often used as a disguise for such 'practical and prosaic' functions.

87 , 88   LE CORBUSIER, *Pessac Housing,* before and after, 1925 and 1969. Ground floors were walled up, pitched roofs were added, the ribbon windows were divided up, terraces were turned into extra bedrooms, and a great number of signs which connoted 'security', 'home', 'ownership', were placed all over the exterior, thus effectively destroying the Purist language. (Architectural Association, Philippe Boudon).

because they felt these historical elements signified lack of creativity. For Frank Lloyd Wright and Walter Gropius the use of historical elements even signified lack of integrity and character. An architect who used the symbolic sign was probably insincere and certainly snobbish – the Classical Orders were a kind of pretentious Latin, not the everyday vernacular of industrial building and sober utility. From these latter building tasks a universal language, they hoped, could be constructed, a sort of Esperanto of cross-cultural usage based on functional types. These signs would be **indexical** (either directly indicating their use, like arrows, linear corridors), or else **iconic**, in which case the form would be a diagram of its function (a structurally-shaped bridge, or even Venturi's duck). Modern architectural words would be limited to these types of sign.

The only problem with this approach is, however, that most architectural words are symbolic signs; certainly those that are most potent and persuasive are the ones which are learned and conventional, not 'natural'. The **symbolic** sign dominates the **indexical** and **iconic**, and even these latter depend somewhat on knowledge and convention for their correct interpretation. There was thus a devastating theoretical mistake at the very base of the modern language. It couldn't work the way the architects hoped because no living language can: they are all based mostly on learned conventions, on **symbolic** signs, not ones which can be understood directly, without training.

A good example of architects' mistaken attitude towards the symbolic sign is their treatment of the pitched roof, which conventionally signifies 'home' in Northern countries. The modern architect disregarded this custom   87
                                                                                                                           88

for functional and aesthetic reasons, to create roof gardens, more space, rectilinear form (Walter Gropius gave six rational reasons for designing flat roofs). Not surprisingly these flat-top buildings were regarded as alien, as insecure, even unfinished and 'without a head'. The houses had been decapitated. Many of the inhabitants of Le Corbusier's Pessac felt his stark white cubical forms lacked a proper sense of shelter and protection, so they shortened the ribbon windows, added shutters and more window mullions; they articulated the blank white surfaces with window boxes, cornices and eaves; and some put on the old Bordeaux sign of protection, the pitched roof. In short, they *systematically misunderstood* his Purist language and systematically redesigned it to incorporate their conventional signs of home.

In spite of the many flat-roofed housing estates today, certain unreconstructed people still go on in their incorrigible way thinking that pitched roofs mean shelter and psychological protection. Many studies have shown this, and a major building society in England, recognising the fact, has taken as its symbol an archetypal couple walking arm in arm under a pitched-roof umbrella. Since this sign exists and since repeated usage will always create the **symbolic** sign, the modern architect might change his attitude towards these conventions. He might regard them as powerful meanings to be used normally in a straightforward way, if only to catch the attention of an audience he wants to convert.

If one wants to change a culture's taste and behaviour, or at least influence these aspects, as modern architects have expressed a desire to do, then one has to speak the common language of the culture first. If the language and message are changed at the same time, then both will be systematically misunderstood and reinterpreted to fit the conventional categories, the habitual patterns of life. This is precisely what has happened with modern housing estates. Pruitt-Igoe and Pessac are the two most celebrated examples. A more promising approach for the modern architect, or social interventionist, would be to study the *popular* house in all its variety and see how it signifies a different way of life for different taste cultures and ethnic groups.

Broadly speaking, these groups are classified in socio-economic terms by sociologists and market researchers, even though there is a lot of overlap and borrowing between groups, and there are other forces at work.[12] The class influence on taste is only one of several influences. It seems to me more exact to speak of semiotic groups than class-based taste cultures, because those groups which share preferences of **meaning** have a life and continuity of their own, which is only lightly coloured by socio-economic background. Basically, semiotic groups are in different universes of signification and have different views of the good life. I will mention three versions of the popular house which spring from these different groups.

1 The ideal of many working-class families is to buy a detached, small house, a bungalow roughly similar to others in an area they know. The values expressed in these houses are security, ownership, separation (a free-standing building), and a kind of conservative anonymity (represented by conforming more or less to the norm of the area). Levittown in America, and the Ideal Home Exhibition in Britain, as well as most buildings in both countries, cater to this semiotic group. It could be called conservative or conformist, sensible or petit-bourgeois,

89
90

89 'POPULAR BUNGALOW', Wales, 1975. Speculative builders have dominated this market since Levittown set the lower middle-class standard. Obvious signs are always incorporated which vary in their sources: Georgian bay window versus rustic stone chimney; plastic shingle versus cottage sign; display of car versus front garden; detached from the group, yet in the style of the neighbourhood. These minor contradictions display just the right blend of personality and conformity.

90 The ETON HOUSE, *Ideal Home Exhibition,* London, 1974. The facial metaphor is often present at the Ideal Home Exhibition, with two or three examples strictly symmetrical about the front door ('mouth'). Various signs of status are tacked on (such as the fibre-glass, Adam detailing), but the snobbism is more apparent than real: it is not meant to convince the neighbours that you sent your son to Eton, but simply to distinguish the building from 'council housing'. This is perhaps the strongest social motivation, the distinction between 'us' and 'them' (those 'controlled' by the government). Hence the Ideal Home styles are relatively permissive, including Swiss Chalet and American Ranch House. In fact for 1976, the Ideal British Home was Colonial, an unforeseen consequence of 1776.

91 KEVIN FISHER, *English Popular House Analysis,* 1976. This synthesis of several reigning trends in the market shows how eclectic and permissive the popular English house is becoming. A pastiche of Japanese, American and English, modern and traditional, urban and rural. Few architects would dare use such a language because of its impurity, so the market remains open to the speculators. It is of course *possible* to use any language to send any message.

depending on which values are stressed and who is doing the valuing, because all these aspects are very clearly signified in the language. The archetype is a two-storey house with a central doorway, a symmetrical displacement of windows on either side, a chimney and pitched roof — all of which vaguely resembles a face with two eyes (top windows), nose (entrance portico) and mouth (doorway).

The band of planting in front of the house could be the shirt collar or moustache, symbolic 'moat', or 'forest', depending on what other signs are stressed. Since this group often wants to signal its new-found independence, meanings tend to support the old Anglo-Saxon maxim,

'every man's home is his castle' — and the castle may be defended by a picket fence or garden gnomes. There is a stately avenue winding to the front door — the curved pathway; past sylvan forests — bushes.

2   The next semiotic group tends to take the previous values for granted, since it hasn't just left what is regarded as the teeming city. In America this group might be called middle-class fastidious, since the clipped lawns and status signs of colonial provenance (nearly always false) harangue the passerby like some Bicentennial orator in a fit of nationalism. Indeed, cleanliness and caution, hard

92 , 93   LUCILLE BALL'S *House*, Beverly Hills, c. 1955. Movie Star House tourism has been a mass industry since the twenties, and maps are thankfully provided for visiting anthropologists. The habitat and layout of these houses is so conventionalised as to constitute a norm: first a public street and sidewalk, then a layer of manicured verdure discreetly signifying privacy, then the rambling house in one of five acceptable styles; the garage to one side. Behind this the tennis court, swimming pool and shrine room where the star's previous triumphs are shown to invited guests. This screening room often doubles as an exercise and game room, since physical fitness and relaxation are the two major drives of this tribe. The 'California Colonial' of Lucille Ball's house, with its raised eyebrow dormers, is the most popular style, followed closely by pseudo-Tudor. (Carol Barkin and Stephanie Vaughan).

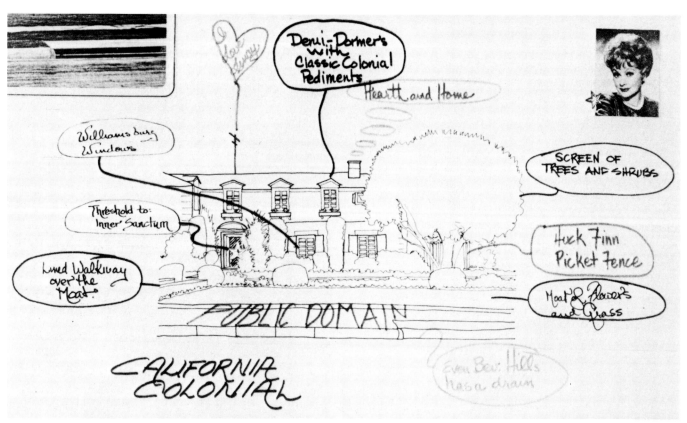

work and discretion, prosperity and sobriety – all the images of WASP success – are there to brand this as the ultimate bourgeois dream. The only problem with this classification is that the appeal of these values reaches much further than the middle class.

92- For instance, the reigning style of movie star houses, those of Beverly Hills and Bel Air which sell from a
95 quarter of a million dollars to three million, fall in this category. The movie stars clearly aren't middle-class, even if their tastes look it and they've come from this background. Are they slumming, or have they just adopted a previously existing semiotic tradition and then amplified

it? Often they are called the 'aristocracy of America', because their values and way of life have become the standard of emulation for the mass of America. Films, and countless sightseeing bus trips going past the stars' houses, (a minor industry since 1922), have made these buildings the most influential in popular taste. They tend to be in one of six styles: **1** Southern Mansion, **2** Old English, **3** New England Colonial, **4** French Provincial/ Regency, **5** Spanish Colonial, or **6** Contemporary/ Colonial Hybrid. These are also the six reigning styles of the popular suburban house. A close investigation will reveal that most of these houses are Ersatz. That is, few of

94, 95 JIMMY STEWART'S *House,* Beverly Hills, c. 1940. A very fastidious mixture of Tudor and Japanese architecture with Swiss accents. The clarity of outline, the black and white alternatives, the very studied informality of massing and planting send out a clear message. Such houses, often exposed in films, have confirmed if not created the American Dream House. Similar examples can be found outside every major city from Boston to Los Angeles, and since the norm is so invariable it almost constitutes a 'language without speech'. Put another way one could say that the language itself does the talking and the designer is a mouthpiece of this language. (Carol Barkin and Stephanie Vaughan).

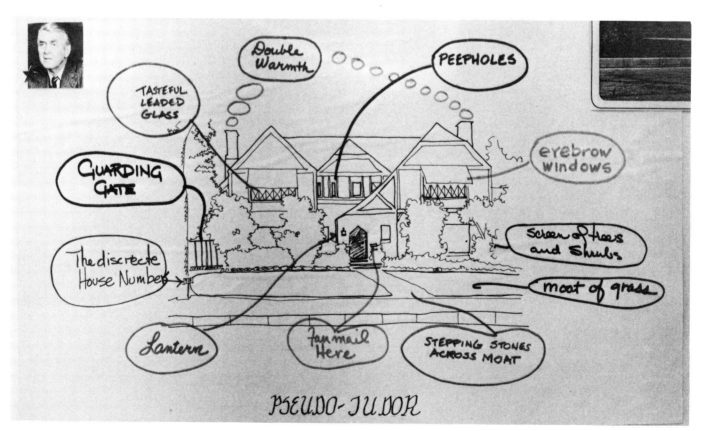

them are serious, scholarly revivals, there is almost no pretence to historical accuracy or serious eclecticism. The styles are notional, **signs** of status and historical roots — but signs meant to remind you of the past, not convince you that the building is living in the present. There are amusing cases when the signs become the whole building itself.

96–98

3   Another semiotic group distinguishes itself from the previous one by inverting these signs and values. A studied casualness is preferred to fastidiousness, a kind of seedy, unselfconscious comfort is preferred to blatant order and rectitude. The down-at-the-heels aristocrat and the intellectual, the drop-out and left wing socialite all unite against what they take to be the vulgarity of the previous group's 'good taste'. Even the modern architect unites with them on this score.

Thus we find the emphasis on nature and **naturalness,** the building isolated and hidden in the actual woods, (as opposed to bushes), which are not manicured to near perfection. They are allowed to grow almost freely, just cut back at certain points to reveal a gable here, a roof there, as if by felicitous chance. In fact it is our old friend the picturesque tradition, the celebration of the carefully

96 , 97   DISSEMINATION of the Movie Star Language, *Gay Eclectic House,* in the lesser side of Beverly Hills, conversion c. 1975. Analysis by Arloa Paquin. In this area interior decorators and others have started to convert their 1930 bungalows. Starting from a 20ft stucco box, they add on a false brick front (in this case), with carport, grillwork and 'false' shingles and Mexican beams. Some of these distortions of the code are amusing. Others are creative, most are cloying; but the language is at least being used (instead of entirely dominating the speaker).

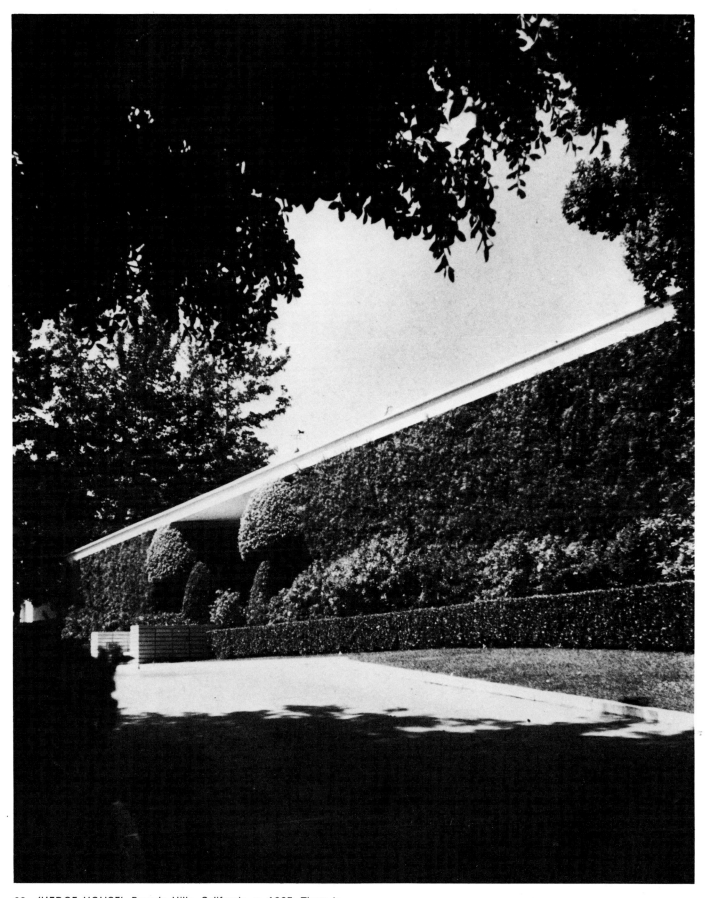

98 'HEDGE HOUSE', Beverly Hills, California, c. 1965. There is nothing much left of the old modern architecture which the owner disliked and covered with various 'natural' signs of planting. These clipped bushes, manicured to fit in the remaining fascia, heighten the act of entry and 'protect' the doorway. They have become conventional signs mandatory for all movie star houses.

careless and studied accident, in a variety of new clothes. These may be the white modern architecture of the 1920s, (*Le Style Corbu* has actually become a popular status-badge when handled by Richard Meier), the stick-and-shed style of the 1960s, or the House and Garden style of the last seventy years, represented on a collective level by such resorts and communities as Port-meirion and Port Grimaud.

Portmeirion is a misplaced Italian hill town set on the lush Welsh coast, surrounded by two miles of rhodo-dendron and other exotic overgrowth. Every vista is carefully composed as a landscape, each path wanders perfectly around every rock outcrop, each bush and flower relates miraculously to near and far buildings, and space ebbs and flows like water into small contained pools and dramatic, open cascades. *Trompe l'oeil*, phoney windows, buildings shrunken to five-sixths of their normal size, eye traps, calculated naivities, whimsical conceits (a sail boat is turned into concrete and thence into a re-taining wall) — this sort of easy-going wit has proven

101 PORTMEIRION, view into Battery Square, showing seaside architecture and Italian campanile. This stage-set architecture has, not surprisingly, been used in several films and commercials. This was the first creation of a formula that was later applied, in a cheap-ened version, to communities such as Port Grimaud, and ride-through parks such as Disneyland.

100 SIR CLOUGH WILLIAM-ELLIS, *The Pantheon,* Portmeirion, 1926–66. A picturesque massing of foliage, and eclectic fragments cannibalised from destroyed monuments. Here an English lantern surmounts a Florentine dome painted day-glo green, which is on top of pink-Palladian walls, which is behind an actual Norman Shaw fireplace (through which you enter!).

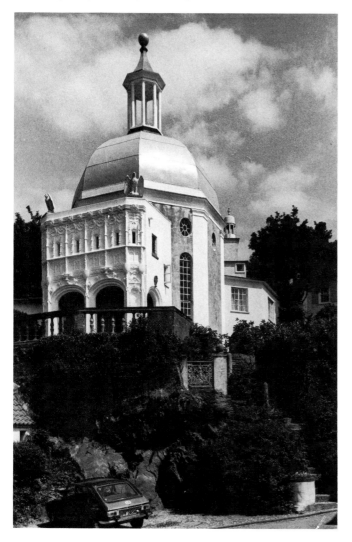

popular with writers and tourists. The builder, Sir Clough William-Ellis, has cannibalised old buildings and pre-served parts of them in his new confections.

This care for the old and traditional is very apparent and one may take it as a characteristic sign of this semiotic group. The ancient is valued not so much for itself, but as a sign of continuity between generations and a con-nection with the past. While the first guess is that such values and understatements appeal only to elite tastes, this does not turn out to be true. For instance, 100,000 visitors

Opposite
99 RICHARD MEIER, *Douglas House,* Harbor Springs, Michigan, 1971–3. The villa in nature, enclosed, protected, and yet standing out as a man-made element. This Italian tradition, taken over equally by Le Corbusier and the upper classes, contrasts the raw and the cooked, the untouched and the finished. Here Meier uses a Corbusian syntax to represent the interior space, which is layered both horizon-tally and vertically through four storeys. (Ezra Stoller).

come to Portmeirion every year, this sophisticated version of Disneyland; and millions visit country houses in England, mostly because of their rich historical associations.

These three semiotic groups, the conservative, the fastidious and the 'natural', hardly exhaust the plurality of taste cultures which exist in any large city. In America there is also the Main Street tradition, which Robert Venturi and Denise Scott Brown have analysed as a series of signs, and England has its counterpart in the High Street.

Venturi, Scott Brown and their team have been instrumental in calling attention to this wide area of symbolism, and have put on an exhibition 'Signs and Symbols of American Life', which has presented some of the images that make up a popular language. Their own design, where possible, incorporates these signs, usually in an ironic and esoteric way. While many critics deplore their work as unnecessarily banal, or ugly, or condescending – that is, anything but popular – their deadpan approach is not necessarily a bad thing. After all, an architect may use a language without sending the customary messages, and if he wants to signify 'the ugly and ordinary' with this

102

103

104

language he has a perfect right to do so. The Venturis justify their approach as social criticism: they want to express, in a gentle way, a mixed appreciation for the American Way of Life. Grudging respect, not total acceptance. They don't share all the values of a consumer society, but they want to speak to this society, even if partially in dissent. Also their sensibility is through and through modernist, their training has been in the language of Le Corbusier and Louis Kahn, so they cannot use popular signs in a relaxed and exuberant way – on a level with the Las Vegas sign artists whom they admire. But how could they? It takes years, perhaps a generation, to master the unselfconscious and conscious use of a new language, and so these architects are, to use a phrase borrowed from the Futurists, 'the primitives of a new sensibility'.

We may expect to see the next generation of architects using the new hybrid language with confidence. It will look more like Art Nouveau than the International Style, incorporating the rich frame of reference of the former, its wide metaphorical reach, its written signs and vulgarity, its symbolic signs and clichés – the full gamut of architectural expression.

102 ROBERT VENTURI, DENISE SCOTT BROWN and TEAM, *The Street,* section from an exhibition 'Signs of Life: symbols in the American City', Renwick Gallery, Washington DC, 1976. Public buildings, state capitols, courts in a classicising style are mixed with the commercial vernacular. This exhibition documented popular symbolism in three major areas: the house, the main street, and the commercial strip. The 'lessons' that these designers drew favoured symbolic instead of sculptural architecture, 'decorated sheds' instead of 'ducks'. (Smithsonian Institution, Washington DC).

103,104 VENTURI and RAUCH, *Tucker House,* Katonah, New York, 1975. The exterior exaggerates elements of the popular code – the overhanging eaves and picture window – while the interior uses the white, planer International Style as a backdrop for Kitsch and other objects. Actually, the fireplace with its round mirror is a miniature of the house, a very witty comment on the traditional idea of aedicules, miniature models and dolls houses. (Stephen Shore).

Syntax

Another aspect architecture shares with language is more mundane than metaphors and words. A building has to stand up and be put together according to certain rules, or methods of joinery. The laws of gravity and geometry dictate such things as an up and down, a roof and floor and various storeys in between, just as the laws of sound and speech formation dictate certain vowels, consonants and ways of speaking them. These compelling forces create what could be called a syntax of architecture – that is the rules for combining the various words of door, window, wall, and so forth. Most doors, for instance, follow the syntactical rule requiring a floor, necessarily flat, on both sides. What happens when this rule is constantly broken? The fun-house at the Amusement Park – which takes advantage of the fact that the nervous system unconsciously knows the syntactical rules and enjoys having them broken from time to time. Delirious word-salads, the speech of schizophrenics and poetry, all distort conventional grammar. It is obviously one of the defining characteristics of all sign systems used aesthetically.

105

They call attention to the language itself by misuse, exaggeration, repetition, and all the devices of rhetorical skill.

Michael Graves speaks about 'foregrounding' the elements of architecture by turning them on their side, extending them out from their usual, functional context and painting them like a Juan Gris Cubist composition. His houses are poetic distortions of a Cubist syntax, whose only fault, in terms of communication, is in the choice of a limited syntax and undercoding. You need a reader's guide to appreciate the fact that a blue balustrade is a column lying down. The Handmade Houses of the West Coast use a much more accessible syntax in a similar way. Shingles, wood siding, different types of standard windows tipped on their sides, placed at the corner of the building, roofs pitching at odd angles, logs used without finishing – these syntactical tricks have a richer resonance of meaning, except, of course, for those trained in synthetic cubism. Again it is a matter of coding and richness of coding which is at stake, not an absolute difference in meaning.

The syntax of architecture has preoccupied the modern movement to the point of obsession, which is one reason it will not be emphasised here. Starting with nineteenth-century theorists, Viollet-le-Duc, Semper and Choisy, this interest was soon idolised and became the dominant meaning of architecture. It's as if all that architecture suddenly had to talk about was its constructional process, the way it was put together. Louis Kahn wrote about THE FORM of building as if it were the Architectural Saviour which would rescue him from all other concerns.

Peter Eisenman produces beautiful syntactic knots which dazzle the eye, confuse the mind, and ultimately

109–
111

Opposite above
107 BOOTMOBILE, Los Angeles, 1976.

Opposite below
108 HOT DOG STAND, Los Angeles, c. 1938. Reinforced with additional signs such as oozing mustard, 'Tail-o-the-pup' etc. This architecture would appear to be unambiguous, yet at the Architectural Association in London, where I teach, it is classified in the slide library as a 'hamburger stand'. Once again, visual codes are mainly local. See page 46.

signify *for him* the process that generated them. How enticing; how banal. The spirit of process is supposed to lift you heavenwards so you overlook the prosaic assumptions. Once again, as with Mies, the analogy of beautifully consistent form is meant to stand for the missing values, transport the mind above ordinary concerns. But this Architectural Ascension is not quite miraculous enough; there is no lift-off, that is, syntactically speaking. Semantically, (a mode of communication Eisenman disdains), his buildings convey the sharp white light of rationality and the virtues of geometrical organisation: the exciting 'bridges to cross', surprising punched-out 'holes of space', the framed 'vistas', the Chinese puzzle of structure. So far as one can recognise these semantic meanings and connect them with other associations, (Protestantism, the white architecture of the twenties), then these buildings have a wider meaning. In other words, the pure realm of syntax is only relevant perceptually when it is incorporated into semantic fields.

112
113

Semantics

In the nineteenth century, when different styles of architecture were being revived, there was a fairly coherent doctrine of semantics which explained which style to use

105 EZRA EHRENKRANTZ, *SCSD (Schools Construction System Development)*, California, 1960s. The syntax of architecture obviously relates to functional concerns, as this drawing shows. Six major elements: **1** mixing boxes, **2** rigid ducts, **3** flexible ducts, **4** outlets, **5** lighting, **6** roof plenum, show the air-conditioning requirements. These were combined with roof, floor and a partition system to give a flexible syntax that could be changed in several ways. (Drawing by Mary Banham from *The Architecture of the Well-tempered Environment* by Reyner Banham.)

106 HANDMADE HOUSE, West Coast, c. 1970. Traditional wooden construction and ready-made windows and doors are displaced from their usual syntactic position to, again, call attention to themselves: 'The Window Building'. (From *Handmade Houses, A Guide to the Woodbutcher's Art,* by Art Boericke and Barry Shapiro, 1973. The owner and place are not identified).

Opposite above
109 MICHAEL GRAVES, *Benacerraf House addition*, Princeton, 1969. A Cubist syntax is used to call attention to itself. This heightening of our perception of doors, stairways, balustrades and views from a terrace is complex and masterful. It is so rich here that one forgets to ask what the functions are (actually an open terrace above, and a playroom and breakfast room below). Note how the structure, sometimes unnecessary, is pulled away from the wall. Railings and cut-out wall planes also serve to define a net of rectilinear space. The front balustrade is, conceptually, a column lying on its side – a play on syntactical meaning, as is the whole addition. (Laurin McCracken.) See page 64.

Opposite below left
110 MICHAEL GRAVES, *Hanselmann House*, Fort Wayne, Indiana, 1967–8. The entrance to this house is heightened, literally by being raised, and metaphorically by the foreground stair, the direct frontal approach, and various articulations over or near the actual doorway. Thus the act of entry, a procession across a bridge and then through a series of layered spaces, is given an almost sacred significance. Views of trees and sky are also heightened by frames, or curved soffits. The curved railing, the extended three columns and the diagonal (stair) all call attention to syntactic features.

Opposite below right
111 MICHAEL GRAVES, *Snyderman House*, Fort Wayne, Indiana, 1972. The intersection of two related syntaxes, Corbusier and Rationalist, set up actual semantic meanings: e.g. 'a war between a Mondrian and a Juan Gris', 'a stucco building trying to spring out of a prison cage', 'a collision of two ships', 'scaffolding' etc. This elaboration of a 1920s syntax is Baroque in every way but the curvilinear.

112, 113 PETER EISENMAN, *House III* for Robert Miller, Lakeville, Connecticut, 1971. Several of the drawings which generated the house show the main oppositions between two grids at 45° (step 6), a conceptual cage of boxed space (step 7), a column grid (step 3), and wall planes in 'shear' (step 5). Bridges and open volumes unite and divide the room functions. The facades 'mark' some interior transformations, that is if you look at them with the diagrams in your hand and think for a long time. This architecture, like nineteenth-century programme music, demands a complementary text in order to be fully understood.

114 J. C. LOUDON, *How to Dress a Utilitarian Cottage,* sketches
from Loudon's *Encyclopaedia.* A basic cube with hipped roof is
transformed with verandah and terrace, with trellis, with a castellated
Gothic jacket, monastic habit and Elizabethan front. The suitability
of style depends on the owner's role and place of residence.

115 THOMAS USTICK WALTER, *Moyamensing Prison,* Philadelphia, 1835. The Egyptian style, with its battered walls, heavy columns and small openings, naturally signified a structure from which it was hard to escape. (HABS, Library of Congress, photo Jack E. Boucher).

on which building type. An architect would pick the Doric Order for use on a bank because the Order and the banking function had certain overtones in common: sobriety, impersonality, masculinity and rationality (a bank was meant to look tough enough to discourage robbers, and sensible enough to encourage depositors). Not only were these semantic properties set by comparison, by looking at the Orders in opposition to each other and other styles, but so were a host of syntactic aspects: the size of the Doric capital, the column's relation to other columns, and its proportion to the cornice, frieze and base. Since these forms and relationships were used coherently, people felt able to pass judgement on their *suitability.* They could tell what the building signified, and they could read a slight change in emphasis, a variation of proportion, as a change in meaning.

Of course, this is to idealise the situation, as only a small part of the community could make these distinctions. But at least *some* could, and this community (echoing the root-word 'communication') kept the architect responsive to the whole enjoyable game of signification. He knew that if the semantic system were violently overthrown or became too complicated, his communication would be reduced to primitive gestures. In fact, by 1860 the game of eclecticism had become too complicated. For this reason it was overthrown, and vilified sixty years later because it had failed to signify those meanings architects found

important. But it needn't have broken down if an adequate theory of eclecticism had been in operation. (I can't discover anything of that time that develops much beyond the notion of syncretism: taking the best parts from different buildings and combining them).

Nonetheless, revivalist architects did at least justify their choice of a style in terms of appropriateness, suitability; and this gave a degree of coherence to their formal choice. One architect, J. C. Loudon, proposed a theory of 'associationism' based on the notion of 'association of ideas', and even went so far as to say that each house should convey in its manner the character and role of its owner.[13] If the inhabitant were a country parson, the house should be dressed in castellated Gothic or related 114 clothing. Thus the environment would become more and more legible as society became more differentiated.

To a certain extent this doctrine was followed in the nineteenth century, and you find that the introduction of a new style is assimilated into the appropriate semantic field. The Neo-Egyptian Style, popular in 1830 because of the Rosetta Stone and Napoleon's previous campaigns, was used sensibly on banks, tombs, prisons and medical 115 colleges. The argument for its use might be based either on **conventional** or **natural** meanings. In the first cases, Neo-Egyptian was appropriate because the Pharaohs buried their treasure in temples of this style; or famous Egyptian doctors, healers and practitioners of medicine were sometimes also architects. Hence by the association of ideas, you could properly use the Egyptian style on banks and chemists' shops. Secondly, this style had natural meanings of heaviness, impenetrability and massiveness. The walls are battered and the openings small — use it on prisons, it 'naturally' signifies high security.[14]

116 CHARLES GARNIER, *Paris Opera House*, 1861–74. The giant, heroic order is played double height against a smaller one. Surfaces are covered with sculpture and polychromy. Everywhere statues take up operatic poses, flexing their muscles — even the women look intimidating. The interior grand staircase displays people as if they were to make an entrance on stage. The internal corner, with its re-entrant angles, medallions and general grandiloquence, is the most musclebound corner of the time. The Second Empire style *naturally* signified power: it took a lot of money to build. (French Government Tourist Office).

By the same line of reasoning, the Neo-Baroque, or Second Empire Style of 1860 had a series of natural overtones. It was massive, overarticulated, splendiferous, muscular, angst-ridden, tempestuous, bombastic, playful, exuberant, pretentious, and very expensive to build. Where should it be used? On the opera house of course. Garnier's Parisian confection of the 1870s was most suitably clothed; and it was no accident that when he conquered France, Hitler danced a jig on its steps. His choice of this style for the Third Reich (an Empire meant to last longer than the French attempts) was both appropriate and inadvertent. It symbolised strength, but like so many governments which have chosen this style, it was a strength that didn't survive its leader. Today, for this historical reason, it conventionally symbolises 'vanished power' or 'ineffectual dictatorship', and is used in innumerable movies and television dramas to signify this ambivalent pathos. The short-lived nature of the architectural code, and its distortion by historical events thus brings out once again the domination of conventional meaning over natural signification.

We can clarify this issue by looking at the classical language of architecture, the way the Three Orders constituted a semantic system, and how this system changed under the pressures of eclecticism. Vitruvius characterised the Doric Order as bold, severe, simple, blunt, true, honest, straightforward, and in sexual terms, masculine. In part this characterisation stemmed from the natural metaphors inherent in this form, but also it stemmed from historical accident (or at least Vitruvius' account of the Doric Order's birth).

The Corinthian Order was, by contrast, delicate, dainty, slender, ornamental and, sexually speaking, a young virgin. As one would guess, the middle Order, the Ionic, was a kind of architectural hermaphrodite, a neuter — in fact for Vitruvius, a matronly Order, because it was slightly more feminine than masculine (with volutes that look elegant). But these characterisations really only begin to make sense, as E. H. Gombrich has pointed out, when the Orders are put *in opposition to each other*.

> The rigid orders of ancient architecture would seem to be a fairly recalcitrant matrix for the expression of psychological and physiognomic categories; still it makes sense when Vitruvius recommends Doric temples for Minerva, Mars, and Hercules, Corinthian ones for Venus, Flora, and Prosperina, while Juno, Diana, and other divinities who stand in between the two extremes, are given Ionic temples. Within the medium at the architects' disposal, Doric is clearly more virile than Corinthian. We say that Doric expresses the god's severity; it does, but only because it is on the more severe end of the scale and not because there is necessarily much in common between the god of war and the Doric order. (E. H. Gombrich, *Art and Illusion*, London, 1960, pp. 316–317.)

Clearly there is nothing in common between warfare and the Doric except with respect to comparable things or elements: they each occupy equivalent semantic zones. In other words, if we map the Three Orders in a semantic space, it is the relationships (r1, r2, r3) which really matter, and not the 'natural' meanings of the forms, nor the particular semantic axes we choose, (whether Vitruvius' or our own).

As long as we can distinguish clear differences between elements, it doesn't matter too much what these dif-

117 CHARLES GARNIER, *Paris Opera House*, 1861–74.

ferences are, because custom and usage will first set them in one semantic space and then transform them to another. This can be seen in the nineteenth century with the rapid shift of stylistic meanings. For instance, in very crude terms, the concept of state power was indicated successively by the Roman revival, the Greek neo-Classical, the Gothic (at least in the House of Parliament), the Italian High Renaissance, the *Rundbogenstil*, the High Victorian Gothic, and finally in the 1870s, the Second Empire Style. There was a general trend in this evolution towards more and more bombast and articulation, understood metaphors of power; but all of a sudden the semantic system could be overturned. Simplicity could become a correlate of potency, as it was with the Neo-Classical and the International Style. There is nothing to keep an age from inverting the semantic space of its predecessors. The relation of form to meaning is mostly conventional.

We can see this transformation of meanings in the jump from the Classical Language of architecture to Eclecticism, and in the work of one man. Nikolaus Pevsner has summarised the way John Nash used a different 'style for the job'.

> [Nash] had a nice sense of associational propriety; as shown in his choice of the neo-Classical for his

71

118 JOHN NASH, *Chester Terrace*, Regents Park, London, 1825. The Corinthian Order, triumphal arches, and endlessly repeated white forms were used on these town houses giving them an appropriate impersonality and rectitude. The detailing was notional and symbolic, quickly conceived for spec builders. For this kind of opportunism Nash was damned by the serious classicists. C. R. Cockerell: 'Greek bedevilled . . . scenographic tricks hastily thought, hastily executed . . .' The indictment may have its point, but still Nash's willingness to change to the appropriate semantic system has its greater point.

town house and of the Gothic for his country mansion (complete with Gothic conservatory). Moreover, he built Cronkhill in Shropshire (1802), as an Italianate villa with a round-arched loggia on slender columns and with the widely projecting eaves of the Southern farmhouse (Roscoe's *Lorenzo Medici* had come out in 1796); he built Blaise Castle, near Bristol (1809) in a rustic Old-English cottage style with barge-boarded gables and thatched roofs (one is reminded of the *Vicar of Wakefield*, Marie Antoinette's diary in the Park of Versailles, and Gainsborough's and Greuze's sweet peasant children), and he continued the Brighton Pavilion in a 'Hindu' fashion, just introduced after 1800 at Sezincote in the Cotswolds where the owner, because of personal reminiscences, insisted on the style. 'Indian Gothic' . . . (Nikolaus Pevsner, *An Outline of European Architecture*, Harmondsworth, 1964, p. 378.) In effect, Nash has substituted a revival style for each of the Three Orders. Roughly speaking, Hindu has been substituted for Corinthian, Gothic for Ionic and Classical for Doric (the Old English and Italian styles occupy new niches).

More significantly, a single form has taken on its opposite meaning in the system. The Corinthian (or Nash's Classical Order) has become masculine, simple and straightforward, because now it is set against other formal elements. This inversion is a good illustration of the semiotic rule that it is relationships between elements which count more than their inherent meanings. We could find countless other examples throughout architectural history: the Picturesque aesthetic being 'functional' in 1840 and 'anti-functional' in 1920; simple, Platonic forms symbolising truth and honesty in 1540 and deceit and artifice in 1870, and so on. Although our intuition and perception of form may feel straightforward and 'natural', it is based on an elaborate set of changing conventions. It is the differences between juxtaposed elements which constitute one of the bases for their meaning – not the natural overtones inherent in the elements themselves.

Even though aesthetic and technical issues dominate architects today, they still pay some measure of attention to semantics. An architect will use a curtain wall for an office building, because glass and steel feel cold, impersonal, precise and ordered – the overtones of methodical business, rational planning and commercial transactions.

121

120

122

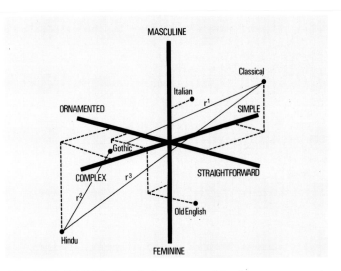

119 The THREE ORDERS. I have used these particular axes of Vitruvius for the sake of simplicity and comparison with the subsequent diagrams. But more interesting oppositions could be chosen as long as they are semantically distinct enough to give different information from each other. For instance, 'nature' might be opposed to 'culture', 'power' to 'impotence', etc. Semantic meaning consists partly in *oppositions within a system*.

120 JOHN NASH'S *Five Styles* compared in the same semantic space as the Three Orders (128). The comparison brings out the fact that it is the *relationship* between styles, or Orders, which matters most in determining semantic meaning. The Corinthian, or Classical Order, has thus taken on its exact opposite meaning in Nash's system, because now it is more masculine, simple and straightforward than the Hindu style.

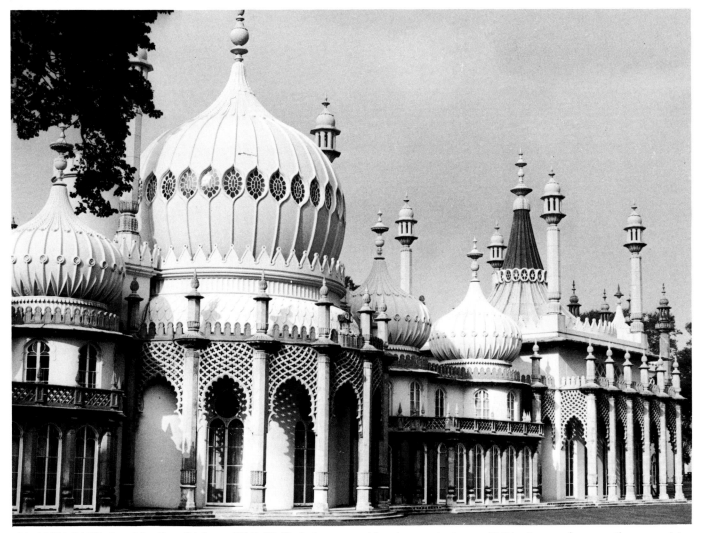

121 JOHN NASH, *Royal Pavilion*, Brighton, 1815–18. Nash threw into his soufflé a bit of Gothic, a bit of Chinese, a bit of cast-iron (palmtree columns), and his own version of a bulbous Hindu style. The domes are faintly mammarian. Here is the beginning of modern Ersatz, the first exuberant Kitsch building in England. Bad taste has been a positive creative force since then reaching one high with the Victorian country house. All this obscures, however, the appropriateness of choosing the Indian style for an escape palace next to the sea. If you are designing a 'pleasure dome' for the Prince who wants to get away from London sobriety, what better than the style of Kubla Khan (published 1816) ?

122 NORMAN FOSTER, *Willis Faber Office,* Ipswich, 1975. Dark
tinted solar glass and steel studs make this 'Big Black Piano' or
'Rolls-Royce' semantically fitting for cool office work. The building
curves around the site, takes up the street lines and reflects the
surrounding environment in fragments. (John Donat).

123 TRADITIONAL SWISS CHALET 'Montbovon', sixteenth-century, now in Geneva. The natural qualities of wood make it semantically suitable for the house. The knots, grain and texture are all metaphors for the wrinkles and birth marks on skin; the surface is tactile, warm and faintly responsive, again like the human body: the material can be easily tooled at a human scale. In this case the surface is adorned with jewellery and decorated like a peasant costume.

One could argue that the architect should deflect these meanings, that business might be made to look more adventurous and domestic than it is; yet the basic classification is suitable.

Wood is intrinsically warm, pliable, soft, organic, and full of natural marks such as knots and grain, so it is used domestically or where people come into close contact with the building. Brick is associated by use with housing, and is inherently flexible in detail, so it is also used domestically. In spite of the fact that there are much more economic building systems available, the wood-and-brick hybrid still accounts for seventy-five per cent of speculative and council housing in Britain – a clear indication that semantic issues take precedence, in the public's mind, over technical ones.

What about new materials such as nylon, which make up pneumatic buildings? The inflatable system is naturally pudgy, squashy, cuddly, sexual, volumetric and pleasant to touch, so it has naturally found a secure niche in the semantic field and is used appropriately on swimming pools, blow-up furniture, entertainment areas and other unmentionable places. Its occasional use as a church or office building brings out different, less dominant semantic overtones.

123

124-
126

124 PAUL BURROWS, Brothel for Oil Men in the Desert, 1973. The pneumatic architecture takes up and supports the natural metaphors of these girls, as well as their activity.

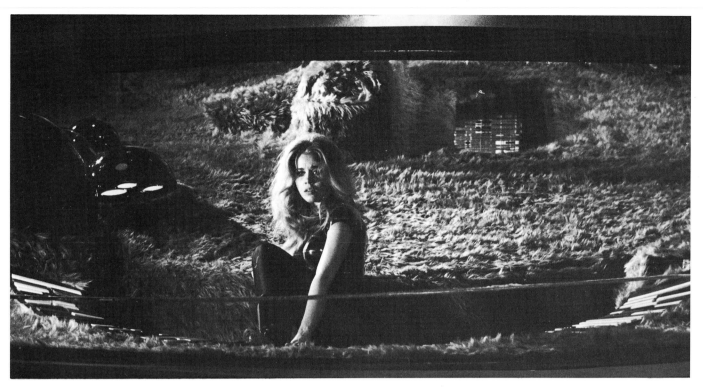

125 BARBARELLA, 1968, is always shown surrounded with viscous, shiny plastic and soft, hairy fur. (ALA Fotocine).

126 JAMES BOND and TIFFANY CASE in *Diamonds Are Forever*, 1971, frolic around on a transparent water bed surrounded by 3,000 tropical fish. Connery's sardonic smile suggests he has had almost enough of this sort of thing. (United Artists).

These comparative aspects of building systems can be graphed in a semantic space similar to that already used, although axes other than the ones I have taken over from Vitruvius would be more relevant. The **relations** between brick, pneumatics, concrete and steel set up the semantic field which will differ slightly for each individual and particular usage employed. Architects do not at present consciously map materials to each other, and functions to each other, and then compare the two mappings. Rather they leave semantic questions to intuition, if they acknowledge them at all. Yet if our complex urban environments are to speak coherently, an explicit method must be used. The various building systems, the new materials, the five or so reigning styles, create such semantic richness as to generate confusion. So far architects have only responded to this as a positive aesthetic gain, trading off stylistic options for psychological and social meaning. As a result no one expects to understand a building and read it as a text. Everyone is the loser, the architect and public. Hence the plea that some system of semantic ordering be explicitly used. It can be as crude as the one proposed here, because it is gross distinctions and oppositions that are at stake, not the fine shades of semantic meaning (which can in any case only be communicated in language).

Several architects have made hesitant steps in this direction — hesitant because they are not backed up by theoretical understanding, or by more than single instances in their large output. One such building in Rome completed in 1965 has been rather heavily criticised for being made up of clichés, and for being schizophrenic. This building, by the Passarelli brothers, uses the conventional forms for office: smooth black steel and glass, below conventional signs for dwelling — hanging vines, broken silhouette, picturesque massing and balconies. A third building system below ground, in monolithic, Brutalist concrete, is the parking garage. The standard joke was that each of the brothers designed a different part of the building and never talked to each other. Part of the criticism directed against this building was for its obvious, boring use of styles already better developed by Harrison and Abromovitz, Paul Rudolph, and Le Corbusier; and one can see the point of this censure.

But also, and perhaps a more deep-rooted reason for the pique was the use of various structures and materials. Architects and critics brought up with the International Style were ingrained with the Purist notion that one aesthetic and structural system should be used on a building. Attendant ideas supporting this were the notions of harmony, the classical ideal that a part cannot be added or subtracted without disturbing the integrated whole, and that each building had, Platonically speaking, one and only one best solution.

There were even further assumptions which this building called into question: the self-conscious use of opposite styles *as styles*. Le Corbusier had said, 'the "styles" are a lie'. Frank Lloyd Wright and Walter Gropius believed that a single style, expressing the character and integrity of the architect, must animate all his work — otherwise he was guilty of insincerity, pandering to the whims of a client and ultimately to a corrupt ruling taste. Eclecticism meant slick facility and lack of conviction.

There are two obvious problems with this single-style approach (still the reigning one, even if it is less explicit than at previous times). First, mixed styles are an aid to communication, as the Passarelli building shows; and an

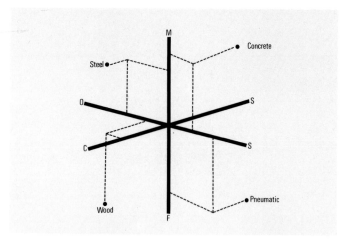

127 FOUR BUILDING SYSTEMS. Particular uses of each building system have to be established before these relationships can be plotted: e.g. the particular use of concrete may in fact be more complex and feminine than the use of steel. Then the functional aspects have to be mapped in the same semantic space, and the two mappings compared.

128 ARCHIGRAM, *Bournemouth Scheme,* 1971, uses four different building systems semantically: the tent-like forms signify ephemeral beach activity, the wandering stepped forms signify large-scale collective activity (department store), the fragmented individual objects are the conventional sign for amusement park, and the linear spine classifies circulation. These sytems are then modified or distorted to articulate further meaning: the linear spine indents to accept plastic pod-like rooms and changes into a lattice girder as it goes out over the water.

architect must master at least three or four to articulate any complex building today, especially if he is to design the interior.

Secondly, the connection of any particular style with sincerity, whether it is the International Style or the *ad hoc* aesthetic of Handmade Houses, is a matter of history and convention, not something eternally true. By that typical process of historical inversion, we have actually arrived at a position where consistency and Purism do not equate with integrity, but quite the reverse. How has this happened?

Precisely because the International Style has been accepted on a massive scale by those who build cities. It is now the conventional style of the ruling class and its bureaucracy, (at least for its large-scale offices and civic

WORLD

SCHIZO

The split functions of mixed development have rarely, if ever, been expressed in so split-minded a way as in the *casa per uffici e abitazioni* recently completed in the Via Romagna at Rome, 1, designed by the three brothers Passarelli: three floors of parking out of sight below ground, an open ground floor concourse, three office floors of the sleekest curtain walling in black steel following the street lines, and finally four floors of crazily expressed hanging gardens punched askew. Rudolph stands on Mies. The quadruple columns (ducts running centrally between them) stand proud as pilotis, are enveloped in curtaining and are threaded through balconies. The obvious merit of this mixture aesthetically is that it develops the accrued confusion of history: Roman wall, neo-Romanesque church, 2, shuttered palazzos. Like so many Italian schemes, it all seems balanced, even academic, in section, 3. How was it designed? Perhaps the brothers split it: Vincenzo the flats, Luca the offices and Fausto the car park—a new Adelphi.

129 PASSARELLI BROTHERS, *Multi-use structure,* Rome, 1965. The concrete and hanging vines classify the flats, the black steel curtain wall indicates office, and below ground, exposed concrete articulates parking. Termed 'Schizo' in this item by *Architectural Review*, and attacked by modernists for its impurity, the building nonetheless makes basic distinctions which are obscured in Purist design.

buildings), so its use hardly ensures that same sincerity which preoccupied the pioneers of the style. Furthermore the 'Masters of Modern Architecture' (I take the phrase from a series of books) have become like the consumer products Coca-Cola, Xerox, and Ford, each with their own house style and corporate brand image. They did not intend this of course, but since they couldn't advertise and since they had to work within a consumer society, the main way of selling their reputation was to develop a single recognisable style which could be purveyed through magazines, books and TV. In short, their authenticity, and their sincerity itself, became a marketable commodity, just as that of Picasso and Ché Guevara did in other fields.

The followers of the 'masters' are led in the same direction, with the result that we can now recognise the Safdie style, the brand marks of Kurokawa and Tange, the Stirling manner, and so forth. How does a client or committee know which one to pick? They choose from books or articles which show his style distinguished from those of competitors. Originality and distinctiveness are saleable items.

The result of this hidden process, of the marketing of reputations, has been to produce a recognisable style of the elite, middle-class architects: it tends towards univalence because of the pressures toward consistency. It is made up from repetitive geometrics, divorced from most metaphors except that of the machine, and purged of vulgarity and the signs common to semiotic groups

130 PAOLO SOLERI, *Arcosanti,* Cordes Junction, Arizona, 1972–7. Restaurant block and accommodation to left and bell foundry and great arch to the right, with housing on either side (semi-circular windows). The Roman-like pattern making, squares, circles and flat masonry walls, is not tied to any semantic system, either historical or internal to the scheme. The formal play is pleasurable, but it doesn't relate to anything other than the grand ecological dreams of Soleri.

other than that of architects. The environment which is created by such a situation is one where every building is a monument to the architect's consistency, rather than appropriate to the job or the urban setting.

The issues involved are obviously complex. An architect must, to a certain extent, develop his own way of doing things, his own details and mannerisms; but these no longer guarantee or signify authenticity as they tended to do before the avant-garde was incorporated into consumer society. And if this practice now produces essentially boring, idiosyncratic sculpture, oversimplified in a single language, then today the architect's sincerity can be measured by his ability to design in a plurality of styles. Consistency equals unconscious hypocrisy, (or, occasionally, conscious elitism).

130

EVOLUTIONARY TREE

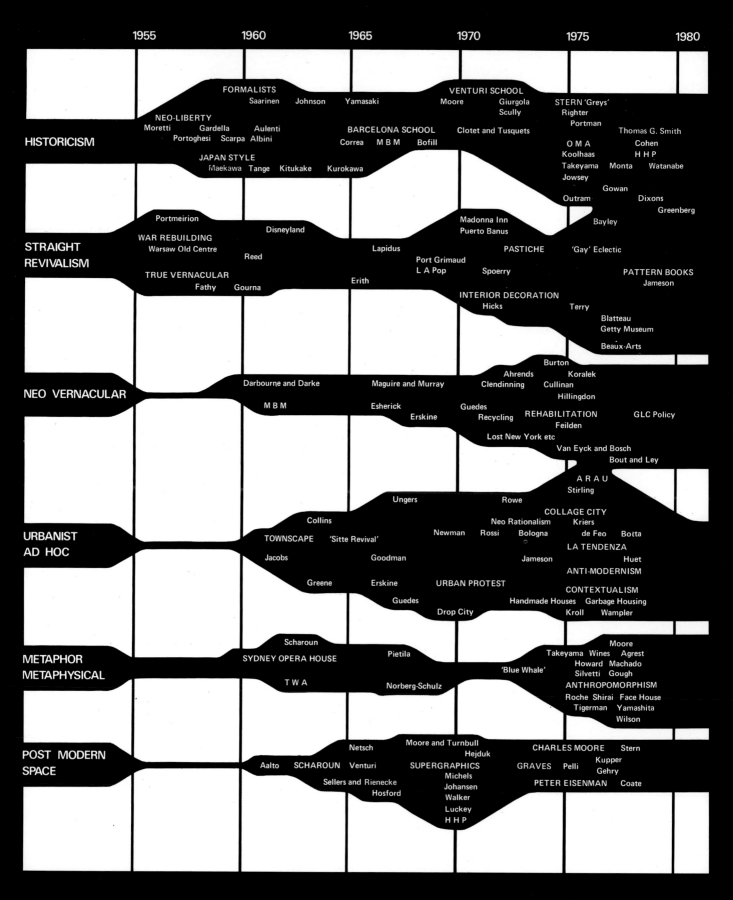

1955 1960 1965 1970 1975 1980

HISTORICISM

FORMALISTS
Saarinen   Johnson   Yamasaki
VENTURI SCHOOL
Moore   Giurgola
Scully
STERN 'Greys'
Righter

NEO-LIBERTY
Moretti   Gardella   Aulenti
Portoghesi   Scarpa   Albini
Portman

BARCELONA SCHOOL
Correa   M B M   Bofill
Clotet and Tusquets

Thomas G. Smith
Cohen
O M A   H H P
Koolhaas
Takeyama   Monta   Watanabe
Jowsey

JAPAN STYLE
Maekawa   Tange   Kitukake   Kurokawa

Gowan
Outram   Dixons
Greenberg

Portmeirion   Madonna Inn   Bayley
Puerto Banus

Disneyland

**STRAIGHT
REVIVALISM**

WAR REBUILDING
Warsaw Old Centre   Lapidus   PASTICHE   'Gay' Eclectic
Reed   Port Grimaud   PATTERN BOOKS
L A Pop   Spoerry   Jameson

TRUE VERNACULAR
Fathy   Gourna   Erith   INTERIOR DECORATION
Hicks   Terry
Blatteau
Getty Museum

Beaux-Arts

Burton
Ahrends   Koralek
Clendinning   Cullinan
Hillingdon

NEO VERNACULAR

Darbourne and Darke   Maguire and Murray

M B M   Esherick   Guedes   REHABILITATION   GLC Policy
Erskine   Recycling   Feilden

Lost New York etc

Van Eyck and Bosch
Bout and Ley

A R A U
Stirling

Ungers   Rowe

COLLAGE CITY
Collins   Neo Rationalism   Kriers
Newman   Rossi   Bologna   de Feo   Botta
TOWNSCAPE   'Sitte Revival'
LA TENDENZA

**URBANIST
AD HOC**

Jacobs   Goodman   Jameson   Huet

ANTI-MODERNISM

Greene   Erskine   URBAN PROTEST   CONTEXTUALISM
Guedes   Handmade Houses   Garbage Housing
Drop City   Kroll   Wampler

Moore
Scharoun   Takeyama   Wines   Agrest
SYDNEY OPERA HOUSE   Pietila   Howard   Machado
'Blue Whale'   Silvetti   Gough

**METAPHOR
METAPHYSICAL**

T W A   Norberg-Schulz   ANTHROPOMORPHISM
Roche   Shirai   Face House
Tigerman   Yamashita
Wilson

Moore and Turnbull
Netsch   Hejduk   CHARLES MOORE   Stern
Kupper

**POST MODERN
SPACE**

Aalto   SCHAROUN   Venturi   SUPERGRAPHICS   GRAVES   Pelli   Gehry
Michels
Sellers and Rienecke   Johansen
Hosford   Walker   PETER EISENMAN   Coate
Luckey
H H P

PART THREE
Post-Modern Architecture

Historicism, the Beginnings of PM

131 The question of what period of architecture might be plausibly revived was fiercely and rather uncharitably debated by the English and Italians in the late fifties. Reyner Banham and his teacher Nikolaus Pevsner launched quite different kinds of attacks on Italian Neo-liberty and what they took to be a return to Historicism (not to be confused with Karl Popper's use of this term in politics). Professor Banham, calling the class to order, attacked 'The Italian retreat from Modern Architecture' as 'infantile regression', because it went back to a pre-machine age style. Pevsner listed the other retreats from the faith and found shades of deviant 'neo-Art Nouveau and neo-De Stijl', neo-this and neo-that sprouting everywhere like poisonous weeds. Their articles and attacks, lasting from 1959 to 1962, were meant to wipe out these heresies with a little critical weed-killer, but in the event the Italians fought back at this Puritanism, the refrigerator school of criticism.[15]

The kind of buildings which were provoking this debate all had vague or repressed historical allusions: Franco 132 Albini's museums and Rinascente, 1957–62, were reminiscent of traditional Roman building; the Torre Velasca,

Milan, 1957, looked somewhat like a medieval tower; Luigi Moretti used an actual rusticated base in the Casa del Girasole, Rome, 1952, while Lubetkin, in England, used, ironically, a caryatid *porte-cochère* as early as 1939. 133 One of the most convincing historicist buildings of the fifties was Paolo Portoghesi's Casa Baldi, 1959–61, an 134 essay in free-form curves definitely reminiscent of the

133 LUBETKIN and TECTON, *Highpoint II,* Highgate, 1938. Because of local hostility to modernism, the architects, half-ironically, incorporated casts of the caryatid removed from the Erechtheum. The classical reference was perhaps fitting to their ordered, classical geometries, but at this stage in time it is the presence of the human figure and the representational boldness, where it is appropriate – at the door – which are noteworthy.

132 FRANCO ALBINI and FRANCA HELG, *Rinascente Department Store,* Rome, 1957–62. A modern *palazzo* with a heavy cornice and no windows, but corrugated service ducts instead. The exposed steel skeleton takes up the proportions of traditional Roman streets, while the masonry echoes the context. (Oscar Savio).

134 PAOLO PORTOGHESI and VITTORIO GIGLIOTTI, *Casa Baldi 1,* Rome, 1959–61. Half Baroque, half modern in its curves and materials. The wall planes curve to acknowledge windows or doors, or create overlapping focii of space. Unlike later buildings by the same architects, the forms aren't entirely sculptural, but keep semantic memories (eg cornice, building block, closed bedroom). (Oscar Savio).

135 EERO SAARINEN and ASSOCIATES, *Stiles and Morse Colleges*, New Haven, 1958–62. Wandering medieval spaces and the heavy crude masonry of San Gimignano were partly sought because of the neo-Gothic campus of Yale. In retrospect the historicism seems diagrammatic, as homogeneous and scaleless as the modernism it was criticising.

Borromini he was studying, yet also unmistakably influenced by Le Corbusier. Here is the schizophrenic cross between two codes that is characteristic of Post-Modernism: the enveloping, sweeping curves of the Baroque, the overlap of space, the various focii of space interfering with each other *and* the Brutalist treatment, the expression of concrete block, rugged joinery and the guitar-shapes of modernism. I give the dates of this Italian historicism to set it against the slightly later emergence of the same thing in Japan, Spain and America (where critics sometimes claim it happened first). Although Saarinen built his 'orange-peel dome', the Kresge Auditorium and chapel, in 1955, and these were reminiscent of Renaissance and medieval prototypes, it wasn't really until his Stiles and Morse colleges at Yale, 1958–62, in 'peanut-brittle Gothic', that overt historicism 135 arrives. Here we have a conscious medieval layout, picturesque massing, an attention to the local Yale context – in sum the beginnings of a sensitive urban place-making. The detail and massing may be diagrammatic, and slightly cheapskate, but this is the modernist inheritance. Saarinen couldn't quite go the next step and design conventional decoration.

Semi-historicism starts in America, in a big way, about 1960 with the major works of Philip Johnson and the more kitsch variants of Yamasaki, Ed Stone, and Wallace Harrison. Yamasaki and Stone produce their sparkling version of Islamic 'grilles and frills' in 1958 and then 'almost-real-Gothic' in 1962 – at least this is the date of Yamasaki's infamous instant arches (awaiting their cathedral, in Seattle). The historicism is attenuated, embarrassed, half-baked – neither convincing appliqué nor rigorous structuralism – a problem for many of the architects who left Mies setting out for decoration (and never quite arrived).

Philip Johnson is easily the most accomplished and intelligent of this group; indeed he probably thought about the problem of historicism far sooner and longer than other architects. His first, tentative break with Mies was the Synagogue in Port Chester, 1956, on the outside a 142 startling simplification recalling those of Ledoux, on the inside memories of the Soane Museum. These historical 141 quotes are located within a black picture-frame of Miesian steel, and the absence of ornament and content mark it as modernist, so Johnson really like so many others is looking two ways. His writing and sensibility probably outdistance his architecture in contributing to Post-Modernism.

In 1955 the essay attacking 'The Seven Crutches of Modern Architecture' exposed some of the formulae behind which modern architects hid, or tried to escape responsibility for formal choice: for instance the pretence to utility and structural efficiency were two such 'crutches'.[16] Johnson later, in 'The Processional Element in Architecture', 1965, also debunked the spatial rationalisations of the modern movement. Combined with his play with historicist shapes (the redundant segmental arch appears in his Amon Carter Museum, 1961 and Follee 1962) these arguments no doubt pushed the door of history open further.

> Mies is such a genius! But I grew old! And bored! My direction is clear; eclectic tradition. This is not academic revivalism. There are no Classic orders or Gothic finials. I try to pick up what I like throughout history. We cannot not know history.[17]

So by 1961 we have at least a camp, laconic statement in favour of eclecticism. What keeps Johnson from developing this is not only his jocular tone, his preference for

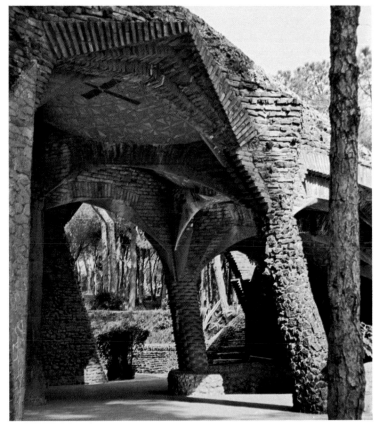

Opposite above
138 RALPH ERSKINE, *Byker Wall on the outside*, 1976, incorporates old buildings into the pattern which is meant to shield the community from traffic noise: multi-coloured brick and ventilator hoods form a kind of syncopated decoration which just avoids being twee. The wall has given great identity to the area, both positive and negative. See page 104.

Opposite below left
139 BERNARD MAYBECK, *Leon Ross House*, San Francisco, 1909. A very dynamic handling of the face theme with all sorts of other ideas going on: a body image, a set of tightly layered frontal planes, the juxtaposition of Gothic and Tudor, the contrast in materials. See page 116.

Opposite below right
140 ANTONIO GAUDI, *Guell Colony Church*, near Barcelona, 1908–15. This entrance porch to the crypt shows the columns leaning and twisting against each other, while the muscles and tendons articulate this dynamic play of forces. Several of the columns resemble the leaning trees, since they are finished with a bark-like stone. The brick domes are hyperbolic parabolas – the whole structure was worked out in model form prior to building. Unfortunately only the crypt was finished. See page 117.

141 SIR JOHN SOANE, *Breakfast Parlour* (*The Soane Museum*), London, 1812. The dome, first secularised by Palladio, is further secularised here in this 'temple' of domesticity. Mirrors take the place of religious iconography, the fireplace replaces the altar, mystical light is replaced by indirect lighting and a very tight, layered space which foreshortens the depth. Soane's work is admired by Post-Modernists such as Charles Moore and Michael Graves. (Trustees of the Sir John Soane's Museum).

142 PHILIP JOHNSON, *Kneses Tifereth Israel Synagogue,* Port Chester, 1956. A thin plaster canopy is stretched tent-like across the nave to break it up into vaulted bays. This use of a traditional compression form in tension, and back-lit, clearly recalls, as Johnson intended, Soane's amazing distortion of classical grammar. (Ezra Stoller).

143 KISHO KUROKAWA, *National Children's Land Lodge,* Yoko-hama, 1964–5. The heavy roof form with upturned eaves, the long horizontals and overlapping construction are all traditional Japanese signs; the proportions and lack of small-scale detail are, however, as modern as the steel tent.

144 KIYONORI KIKUTAKE, *Tokoen Hotel,* Kaike Spa, Yonago, 1963–4. The 'Japan Style' is evident in the constructional elements and the roof restaurant with its gentle curves. In addition the building is highly readable and broken into different semantic areas: board-rooms and conferences rooms at the base, an open deck, two levels of hotel rooms (on the inside proportioned by tatami mats) and the vertical stairway.

surface wit over deeper investigation, but also his very modernist commitment to 'pure form – ugly or beautiful – but pure form.' [18] The historicism of Johnson remains on the level of spotting the source, on esoteric codes rather than on more accessible and conventional ones. He thus never really develops an argument for ornament, regional suitability, or contextual appropriateness – three potential aids to his eclecticism that might have strengthened it.

If Johnson and Saarinen can be classified as semi-Historicist, or one-half Post-Modern (see genealogy, page 80) then so too can the 'Japan Style', and 'the Barcelona School' which develop at the same time, but toward a regionalist expression. The 'new Japan Style', a phrase used by Robin Boyd, is best exemplified in the sixties work of Kunio Maekawa, Kenzo Tange, Kiyonori Kikutake and Kisho Kurokawa.[19] It incorporates nationalist and traditionalist elements within a basically Corbusian syntax. So projecting beam ends, brackets, torii gates, gentle curves, bevelled masts, constructional expression – all the hallmarks of Japanese architecture in wood – are translated into reinforced concrete and juxtaposed according to the method of 'compaction composition'. Le Corbusier developed this method of Cubist Collage, and the Japanese, with their traditional Zen aesthetics of asymmetrical balance, frequently push it toward the refined and exquisite. While they use Brutalist materials and smash them through each other, they still end up with something as elegant as a Tea Ceremony Room (albeit in stained concrete). As with Johnson and Saarinen they remain hesitant about tradition, and wary of a full-blown eclecticism.

'So called regionalism' remarked Tange in 1958, 'is always nothing more than the decorative use of traditional elements. This kind of regionalism is always looking backwards . . . the same should be said of tradition'.[20]

What, might be asked, is really wrong with the decorative use of traditional elements – indeed straightforward ornament and the Trad styles? No one was prepared in the sixties to pose these questions in a radical way, and so the vague modernist suspicion of ornament and convention remained.

143
144

145, 146 ROBERT VENTURI and SHORT, *Headquarters Building*, North Penn Visiting Nurses Association, 1960. The arch, a sign of door, is contrasted with rectangular and diagonal elements, to (over) articulate the public entrance. Traditional decorative mouldings are also distorted on the windows. This bizarre, even 'ugly', usage was nevertheless one of the first buildings which used historical ornament in a recognisable and symbolic way.

147 VENTURI and SHORT, *Headquarters Building,* plan is a distorted box which, on the outside forms an embracing court, and on the inside directs movement with its diagonals. The odd angles and skewed space of Post-Modernism developed from such plans.

I suppose the first *Modern* architect to use the decorative moulding and traditional symbol (such as the doorway arch) in an aggressive way was Robert Venturi. His Headquarters Building for Nurses and Dentists, 1960, has decorative mouldings placed as exaggerated eyebrows over the lower windows, and a paper-thin arch bisected by diagonal struts which shouts out 'public entrance'. All sorts of ideas which were to have later influence are present in this building, so it could be called quite appropriately the first anti-monument of Post-Modernism. Robert Stern was to develop the ornamental ideas and many architects, such as Charles Moore, were to learn from its funny corners, inflected walls, ugly ironies and 'Post-Modern space' (but more of that later). Suffice it to say here that we have finally a building that was wilfully traditional in some respects; like Baroque buildings it was designed in terms of the urban context, the street line and flowing spatial requirements; like a Mannerist conceit it played tricks with scale, bloating certain windows and doors, while diminishing others. Certainly its calculated ugliness and awkwardness were Mannerist: the roof is an insult to the strength of the weather, the boxiness carved up is an insult to the International Style (as it was meant to be).

Robert Venturi's polemics against modernism mostly concentrated at first on the question of taste, and then later on symbolism. In his first book, *Complexity and Contradiction in Architecture*, 1966, he set up a series of visual preferences in opposition to Modernism: complexity and contradiction vs simplification; ambiguity and tension rather than straightforwardness; 'both-and' rather than 'either-or', doubly-functioning elements rather than singly working ones, hybrid rather than pure elements, and messy vitality (or 'the difficult whole') rather than obvious unity. In addition to these stylistic codes, Venturi provided two more important contributions to the growing argument: first was his interest in pillaging from disregarded historical work, such as that of the Mannerists and Lutyens (who now with Gaudí becomes a paragon for nearly all the PMs), and second was his plunge into Pop Art, then Main Street, Las Vegas, and finally Levittown. Along with his wife Denise Scott Brown, and his design team, Venturi looked at these hitherto snubbed manifestations of popular taste for their 'Lessons in Symbolism'. The results were collected in what could be appropriately called the first anti-exhibition of PM architecture, 'Signs of Life: Symbols in the American City' ('anti' because it went against the conventional museum codes of displaying artifacts).

The Venturi argument, taken as a whole, insisted on revaluing commercial schlock and nineteenth-century eclecticism for how they communicated on a mass level. There were certain problems of focus, however: no developed theory of symbolism was put forward, so the examples multiplied every-which-way; no standards for selecting and judging schlock were presented and the argument was conducted on the level of personal taste – not semiotic theory – so that the Venturi 'bill-ding-boards' triumphed somewhat arbitrarily over their 'ducks' (to use two of their fairly primitive categories). In fact the Venturi Team's wholesale commitment to argument by taste and to inverting the taste of the previous generation was exclusivist and modernist at its core.[21] By contrast, Post-Modernism which has developed from semiotic research, looks at the abstract notion of taste and its coding and then takes up a situational position: ie, no

87

148, 149 VENTURI and RAUCH, *Allen Art Museum*, Oberlin College, 1973–7. This addition to an Italian Renaissance revival building of 1917 tries to harmonise and contrast with the previous building through its proportions and pink and red stone. Semantically, however, this 'elegantly decorated shed' is more a gymnasium than a museum, and awkwardly, not gracefully, integrated with its neighbour.

code is inherently better than any other, and therefore the subculture being designed for must be identified before one code can be chosen rather than another.

The Venturi Team would exclude a whole repertoire of codes, not only 'ducks', but also 'Heroic and Original' architecture, the grand gesture, the revival of the *palazzo pubblico*, and all the work they conceive in opposition to their decorated sheds.[22] Why? Because they still keep a modernist notion of the *Zeitgeist*, and their particular spirit of the age 'is not the environment for heroic communication through pure architecture. Each medium has its day'; our day, you might have heard from McLuhan, is one of symbolism via the electronic media – the 'electrographic architecture' of Tom Wolfe. It's amusing to note the symmetrically opposite positions of Team Venturi and Philip Johnson. They both take *a priori* stands on 'pure' form – one anti, one pro – as if such one-sided views of communication were adequate. Since Post-Modernism is radically inclusivist (like Renaissance architecture) it must fault the oversimplification of both polemicists and attack its causes. After all, Modernism is in an important sense nothing but the pretence of one *Zeitgeist* after another, each one claiming to occupy the centre stage, each one swinging the pendulum too far its way, each one adopting the war tactics of shock, slogan and exclusion. A difficulty of Post-Modernism is in adopting plural coding without degenerating into compromise and unintended pastiche, and a way of doing this, as we will see later, is through participatory design, something that subjects the designer to codes not necessarily his own in a way he can respect them.

190–193

The Venturi Team have definitely responded to several codes which have heretofore remained unserviced by architects, those coming from the lower middle class and the commerce of Route 66. Their actual buildings, however, have usually been for a different taste culture – for professors or colleges, or 'tasteful clients' – thus creating a kind of hiccup between theory and practice.[23]

Their practice varies in its commitment to 'ordinary and ugly' architecture. The Oberlin College Addition, 1973–7, is a decorated shed of pink granite and red sandstone – 'a high school gym of the 1940s' as they call it – slammed onto a quietly harmonious Neo-Renaissance building. The juncture, the texture, the roof and pattern are all discordant and calculatedly ham-fisted, and one wonders if the justification – 'the artists don't want architectural heroics' – is enough. There is an obvious jump in logic, caused by their prior commitment to ugliness. For why should the coding of a 1940s high school gym be used? 148-149

The Brant House, 1971, *does* make the argument for its coding by way of association: since the owners have one of the great collections of Art Deco objects, there are various signs of this in the detailing. On the outside, two shades of green-glazed brick slide on the diagonal, and flat streamlines in shiny metal edge the surface. On the inside, taking cues from Lutyens, black and white marble stairs vibrate in opposition and the entrance sequence is punctuated by a series of shifts in axis and scale. 150

But, and again this is where arbitrary coding enters, the back-side is '1930s Post-Office and Walter Gropius', as if those two sources were adequate to Art Deco. Clearly the Venturis are slumming and enjoying the 'dumb' side of things. One more quote brings out the esoteric nature of the codes involved: they say the southern front 'resembles a plain Georgian country house (except there is no central motif)'.[24] Once this comparison is made, however, as with so many other modernist buildings trying to have historical overtones, it is the *non*-historical parallels which dominate. The bow front has expanded to the point that no Georgian would recognise it, as has the gigantic side porch. The windows, colouring, details are all anti-Georgian in their Mannerised proportions. One can enjoy the building for its marvellous idiosyncrasy, for its careful distortion of codes, and its delightful wit – a nice green trellis jumps up the west side – but still wonder why the Venturis have to try so hard at being original in this esoteric way? It's as if their sensibility were still Modernist, while their theory were Post.

Two buildings which are more straightforward in their historical allusions and enjoy an easy-going but interesting commerce with the past, are the Trubeck and Wislocki houses, 1970, which use the Cape Cod vernacular in a conventional yet fascinating way, and the Franklin Court design, 1972–6, a Bicentennial homage to Benjamin Franklin. Here a very appropriate ghost image, in stainless steel, marks the profile of the old, non-existent mansion. Below are the archaeological remains, which can be spied through various bunker-like slits thoughtfully provided above ground. A neo-colonial garden, laid out roughly on Franklin's description, is peppered with various of his morally uplifting slogans. Thus the Venturi Team has produced here not a building, but a very amusing garden which combines meanings from the past and present in a way that isn't excessively idiosyncratic. It's fitting to the urban context, it's within both popular and elitist codes, it's ugly *and* beautiful and thus could be called their first promonument of Post-Modernism. 151

150 VENTURI and RAUCH, *Brant House,* Greenwich, 1971, southern exterior. The green glazed brick in two shades and the metal strips are in tune with the Art Deco collection of the owners, but the intended references to country houses are so oblique and under-coded as to go unnoticed.

151 VENTURI and RAUCH, *Franklin Court,* Philadelphia, 1972–6. An open frame of stainless steel approximates Franklin's old mansion, the 'surprise garden' houses his memorabilia, while the surrounding buildings have been restored – a convincing if modest knitting together of old and new.

152 LLUIS CLOTET, OSCAR TUSQUETS and PER, *Giorgina Belvedere*, Gerona, 1971–2. This belvedere-bedroom is meant to relate to and contrast with the classical estate. You drive in – on the roof – between the temple's colonnade. Double-height space is set off against small-scale trellis and balustrade, and rustic wood shutters against white stucco, a grand irony of Post-Modernism.

153 CLOTET and TUSQUETS, comparison of their belvedere, and 'dog' house in South Africa. Decoration and symbolism here applied with a Venturian literalism.

Perhaps because Robert Venturi and Denise Scott Brown have had to fight Modernism to establish their style and positions, they haven't yet been able to relax with traditional codes, the way their followers have. Clearly Robert Stern, who will be discussed later, has a kind of exuberant facility with the 'Venturi Style', and the Barcelona School can turn it to its local purpose.[25] One group of Barcelona designers, Mora-Piñón-Viaplana, has taken cues not only from Venturi's formal ideas, but also from semiotics in general, to produce ironic juxtapositions of entrance space and circulation, column and wall; while another Team, Clotet and Tusquets, produce a heightened sarcasm by juxtaposing new and old. They place a paper-thin trellis above an heroic order of piers; within the piers and on the roof of the house is the place to park the car surrounded by a balustrade; finally, the piers which come down to the ground act as a screen behind which are rustic shutters and windows – out of phase with the piers. The syncopation of verticals is masterful, the layering of space a surprise, the contrast of meanings a delight. It's rather as if one composed a classical building according to International Style aesthetics (or vice-versa), a typical conceit of Post-Modernism.

With such a building then, finished in 1972, the modern architect *almost* makes his peace with historicism and allows himself to quote tradition directly where it has a purpose (the building is on a classical estate). I underline the word 'almost' because these designers really can't go very far down this traditional road yet, and are fearful of meeting interior decorators and Reactionaries coming back the other way. For this is what has partly stopped their full use of the past – the nostalgia boom, the continuation of reproduction architecture with its Reproduction Furniture, the Traditionalesque Style that never died and often became Kitsch. The ex-modernists still do not want to be tainted with establishment values, the eclecticism that has been the style of wealth and opportunism for the last 200 years. So when they make hesitant steps towards this eclecticism it is always distorted enough to be recognisably still 'modern', structurally at least, the opposite of Kitsch.[26]

Thus Post-Modern architects must distinguish themselves from the next group, those revivalists who never were modern in the first place.

Straight Revivalism
One is often surprised to read how Gothic architecture survived in England through the sixteenth, seventeenth and eighteenth centuries right into the Gothic Revival. It never entirely died because people liked this 'national style', and there were always a few crumbly cathedrals in need of repair. In like manner, the old way of doing things never really stopped. Rather historians stopped looking – except H. R. Hitchcock who called one, small chapter of his contemporary history 'Architecture called Traditional in the Twentieth Century'. Even Hitchcock stops his account in the 1930s and no one, to my knowledge, tries to bring the story up to date in a comprehensive way. The reason for this is partly due to the fact that revivalist styles become kitsch, traditional becomes traditionalesque, and the whole thing a form of ersatz – that is, a clear substitute for the period being revived, neither a very creative extension to tradition nor a scholarly copy.[27] Thus Pittsburgh's 'Cathedral of Learning', a forty-storey gothic cathedral given over to study, or Moscow's seven sky-

154 DAVID HICKS, *Athens Apartment*, 1972. The Doric Order painted white and turned inside-out with a deep frieze which hides the air-conditioning ducts. Chairs and tables are replicated from designs on ancient urns. The white and black graphics are fairly startling in their purity, and more modern than Hellenic.

155 *Moscow State University*, Moscow, 1947–53? Classical realism, the architectural form of Socialist Realism, here borrows the repressive forms of czarism, the stepped pyramids, and the signs of bourgeois power. This coercive and boring symbolism – the architecture of monotony – is tied to an appropriate megalomania: the building houses 18,000 students in a kind of battery-hatch palace. That several western Marxists such as Aldo Rossi admire these buildings as socialist dreams is their luxury; but that they should be offered as urban prototypes is laughable. The insensitivity to context and historical meaning is droll. (Novosti Press Agency).

155 scrapers designed in Stalinist Baroque (or what Intourist guides call euphemistically 'The Fifties Style'). Many such confections were built, and some like the Karl Marx Allée in East Berlin, or the Laboral University in Gijon, are being revalued by Aldo Rossi and others for their urban implications.[28] Rossi and the other Rationalists such as the Krier brothers have stated that, despite accusations, their work is not Fascist; indeed that there is no such thing as an ideological architecture. Their confusions on this score are grandiloquent inasmuch as they also proffer a Communist architecture from time to time.

> [The defamatory critics] are stupid because a 'Fascist Architecture' does not exist. There is, however, an architecture of the Fascist era, Italian or Nazi, just as there is also of the Stalinist era.
> I do have a profound admiration for the architecture of the Stalinist period and I consider today works such as the University of Moscow and the Karl Marx Allée in Berlin, to be among the monuments of modern architecture.[29]

Why? Because they were 'enormous, collective feats' popular with the 'simple people', and they have lessons today for the idea of the street and the monument.

On the positive side, Rossi has contributed to the growing concern for the role of monuments in perpetuating, even defining, historical memory and the image of the city – key ideas for Post-Modernism in coming to terms with the collective, or public realm in architecture. Without a clear insistence on public symbolism – and this means monumental, permanent gestures that self-consciously articulate certain values – the image of a city becomes inchoate, the architecture evasive. But negatively, Rossi fails to understand how symbolism works, why cities and ordinary people have a perfect right to go on calling his architecture Fascist even when he sees and intends it as recalling Lombardy farmhouses and the memories from his childhood. That is to say, once again the architect has no general theory of codes, how they

155

156

28

156 ALDO ROSSI, *Modena Cemetery*, project, 1971. The 'House of the Dead' in the foreground is a literally haunting image. Like a haunted house the windows are blown out and the roof non-existent – perfect for dead people and De Chirico. An empty street leads toward the towering 'common grave', unfortunately coded as a crematorium funnel. This partly inadvertent coding, the overtones of 'the Final Solution', has led to Rossi's popularity and shame. Whether a cemetery should be so remorselessly deadly is open to doubt, but beyond question is the monumental presence, the image of architecture as public memory and symbolism.

are built up through usage and feedback and how they differ according to class and background. Like the Modern architect, he naively just sees the meanings he sees and assumes they, and not other ones, are simply *in* the building. As opposed to this Naive Realism, Post-Modernism acknowledges the all-important contingent nature of meanings. For instance whether Fascism has just used stripped, classical forms or not; and the Post-Modernist then designs with these transitory signs in mind. Of course there is no inherently 'Fascist Architecture', but equally obvious is the fact that recent usage has connected totalitarianism with Neo-Classicism. The Rationalists are trying to resemanticise this form instantaneously as the Fascists did; but it will take another twenty years of new usage before the old is obliterated and they can use it more neutrally.

If time and usage are the crucial variables in architectural meaning, the case of the Straight Revivalists becomes more problematic, for they, like the Modernists are often insensitive to the nuance of time and context. Raymond Erith and Quinlan Terry in England have produced very adequate, scholarly exercises in the classical style – a country house in Kings Walden, Bury, Hertfordshire, that is Adamesque and Palladian, even Georgian in parts. But it was finished in 1971 and there is no indication of this fact other than a kind of wooden propriety in expression.

For a mosque somewhere in the Middle East, Quinlan Terry is producing a dome – 'as big as St Pauls' – but unlike St Pauls flanked by two Indian minarets. Again the drawings are masterful in their attention to light and shadow, and the proportions are nicely inoffensive, but there is no sense of irony in the displacement of cultural forms, or the hiatus in classical design. Although the Modern Movement may have over-simplified and encouraged all sorts of disasters like Pruitt-Igoe, one can't pretend as these designs do, that Modernism never existed. The climate of opinion has to be acknowledged precisely because it is not the *Zeitgeist* that Modernists claimed, but rather a custom like the manners and speech of a nation.[30] It is adopted or honoured out of respect not necessity.

The indifference of the Revivalists on this level is paralleled, it is sometimes claimed, by their lack of creative force, the absence of 'the life of forms' (to use Focillon's expression) in their art. Henry-Russell Hitchcock has pointed out the problem:

> . . . whatever life twentieth century traditional architecture retained as late as the second and even the third decade of the century had departed by the fourth. Post-mortems on traditional architecture have been many – and often premature. The causes of death are still disputable, but the fact of dissolution is by now [1958] generally accepted.[31]

Well Post-Modernism would dispute anything so final as death, and Quinlan Terry has argued the case that the classical tradition, like any other, is potentially alive.

> It is like a three dimensional game of chess – the more you play the game the more fascinating it becomes. When I design I am playing this game; I am not making a pastiche. The designs develop as if they have a life of their own. I find it quite fascinating.[32]

The chess game of working out moves that haven't yet been taken in a tradition is one source of inspiration and life; but contrary to Terry, this may even include pastiche – a rather misunderstood game of the moment.

The respectable design world, the academics and

157 RAYMOND ERITH and QUINLAN TERRY, *Kingswalden Bury*, 1971. Symmetrical temple front is placed in a recessed, diminished entrance. Very slight visual rhythms can just be detected in window bays, but the Palladian exercise lacks any strong underlying idea, or any extension of the classical tradition.

158 QUINLAN TERRY, *Mosque in the Middle East*, 1975– . A classical Roman grammar of centralised buildings with additions of colonial Indian architecture, and for the Middle East! The neo-Classicist is often as insensitive as the modernist in supposing his language to be universally applicable. Terry's buildings, however, do have a fine balance of parts, a human scale and a close-grained texture, as his drawings show.

159, 160 8834 DORRINGTON and 8836 RANGLEY, Los Angeles, c. 1972? Bungalows restyled in various neo-neo-modes by interior designers. The basic eighteen foot box is extended in front by a fence, a hedge, and then stuccoed or veneered facade with various exaggerated signs of status and entrance. But the Neo- styles are mocked with a certain creative wit: note the pediment monsters — lobsters – the disjunction in scale, and the violent contrasts in material. These scenographic tricks are highly readable like all good caricature.

161 MOZUNA MONTA, *Okawa House*, project, 1974. 'The renaissance of the Renaissance', with the outside of the Palazzo Farnese crossed with the inside of the Pazzi Chapel. Since the Japanese, like the Angelenos, rebroadcast culture, and get it slightly wrong, artists such as Monta have taken this parody as their starting point and created serious works based on caricature. The result is sometimes an extension of traditional language.

serious architects, are a little too quick to dismiss this sort of design, but happily there are now several talented semi-designers who are at work in the field. These vary from the Gay Eclectic designers of Los Angeles — the interior 159 decorators who go exterior on their 'Bungaloids' (con- 160 verted bungalows whose sex is changed from 1930s Spanish to 1970s Roccocola and other modes) — to the Japanese architects, such as Mozuna Monta, who consciously travesty the Modern Movement and the Renaissance, making an enigmatic art form out of parody. Toyokaze Watanabe, for instance, bifurcates Le Corbusier's Villa Savoye and Aalto's Town Hall into one building, or builds a colosseum inside an Ottoman castle. Monta, who is the supreme ironist, a man who sees and feels all the cultural confusion of a Japanese living in Western dress — simultaneously in the twentieth and fifteenth century — has crossed various Renaissance proto- 161 types: for instance Michelangelo's Palazzo Farnese with Brunelleschi's Pazzi Chapel. The results of such hybridisation have a certain formal integrity and interest; the game of chess had these undiscovered forms of checkmate inherent in its rules. For a culture, like LA or Japan, which is always copying or essentialising trends a little bit too late, there is an exquisite sweetness to be enjoyed by making this time-lag into a conscious art.

This caricature, or parody of serious culture, of course undermines its pretensions, as the unconscious travesty devalues it. But the subversion is only momentary, a short space of time before the latent humour asserts itself and establishes the travesty as a new level of culture. Monta, Watanabe, Shirai, and to a certain extent Isozaki and Takeyama, are using travesty as a kind of mirror-image genre of cultural confusion, and if it's practised long enough, it may have the unintended consequence of uniting a fragmented society.[33] One of the virtues of parody, besides its wit, is its mastery of cliché and convention, aspects of communication which are essential to Post-Modernism.

Are there moments when Straight Revivalism is appropriate, without any ironies? Conrad Jameson would argue 'yes' when it comes to housing, particularly mass housing, where pattern books are called for.[34] The argument here might be that Georgian or Edwardian terraces work better than modern estates, because a tradition — whichever one it is as long as it is unbroken — contains more values, and well-balanced ones, than a modern architect can invent or design. People enjoy these terraces more than new inventions, they are often cheaper to build than the system-built alternative, and they fit into the urban context, in language and scale. 162 Thus one selects a pattern language suitable to the area and only modifies it piecemeal, if there is need for a garage door here, or a refrigerator there. Otherwise 163 tradition always gets the benefit of the doubt: architecture is a social craft, not a creative art.

While Jameson's arguments are welcome, especially for mass housing, it seems to me they are not as exclusivist as he intends: 'Radical Traditionalism' is just one possible approach among many, and there is no reason an architect can't use it *also* to signal non-social, aesthetic and metaphysical meanings only addressed to the few. Thus Jameson's traditionalism may well be adopted as a leading strand of Post-Modernism, but it will be used as a language which occasionally includes eclectic elements and speaks of personal, even elitist ideas, as well as the social meanings he demands.

162 *Warsaw Old Centre,* rebuilt 1945–53 in replica form based on old photographs, measured drawings and personal accounts of the people who lived there. The market place was rebuilt after the Nazi destruction as a symbol of Poland's rebirth. The interiors were, of course, remodelled in a new way, piecemeal, to suit modern requirements and plumbing. (Embassy of the Polish People's Republic).

164, 165 *Houston Housing Estate,* c. 1971. The fronts are all personalised in one of five pseud styles, while the backs – used for parking and services – are all Bauhaus. A very traditional split between images of decorum and function taken to rather zany lengths.

163 HASSAN FATHY, *Gourna New Town,* Egypt, 1945–7, a rediscovery of the vernacular. This mud-brick village, with its tight protected streets and traditional forms, is an instant recreation of villages that have existed for 2000 years. An example of self-build, the town is not only far cheaper than any modern counterpart could be, but also more varied and delightful. Jameson contends that the architect's role is to rediscover such past building traditions and keep them operative by piecemeal modification. Gourna proves it can be done, but where is the western barefoot architect? (Dalu Jones).

Already there is one strand of commercial revivalism which is a major industry: the popular house and speculator's development. There are also the well-known pastiches of Portmeirion, Disneyland and their world-wide variants. This tradition is developing most quickly in the Far East, Los Angeles and Houston where ersatz new towns, or at least vast housing estates, spring up as fast as a plastic polymer gone berserk. Some communities are so artificial that when you walk in the door for the first time the Van Gogh *Sunflowers* are already hanging on the wall and the concrete logs are crackling out the heat from concealed gas jets. This 'total service' obviously aids a family that has to move every two years and hasn't the time to choose real paintings, and cut the wood. In Europe various ersatz towns are being created, especially by the seashore, such as Port Grimaud, La Galiote, Puerto Banus. When compared with modernist new towns, or even modern seaside resorts, these fabrications are clearly more humane, appropriate and enjoyable – hence their commercial success. Maurice Culot, a *soi-disant* Stalinist, even sees them as the answer for the communist future, a nice irony of hypertensive capitalism being the midwife of history.[35] Whatever 'historic compromises' actually occur over ersatz new towns, it is time architects followed speculators into this field and took advantage of such commercial and social pressures for architectural ends. Both society and architecture would gain from this arranged marriage.

An American example of revivalism, which has elicited all sorts of response from architects and critics, is John Paul Getty's Museum in Malibu, California, a scholarly recreation of Herculaneum's Villa of the Papyri – plus other Pompeian delights. Architects have damned the building as 'disgusting,' 'downright outrageous,' 'too learned', 'frequently lacking in basic architectural design judgement', 'fraudulent', 'recreated by inappropriate technologies' and of course too expensive ($10 million or was it $17, a mere *hors d'œuvre* for Getty). These predictable outcries have been rebutted by David Gebhardt, the incisive historian from Southern California, who,

164
165

166

192

167

166 FRANCOIS SPOERRY, *Port Grimaud,* 1965–9. Drive your sailing boat right up to the manicured lawn of a Provencal fishing village in reinforced concrete. No two houses are the same, and the variety of spatial experience is well above the modernist counterpart, leading this village to become the major model for resort centres in the Mediterranean. Several Far Eastern versions are planned . . .

167 *Getty Museum,* inner peristyle garden. False windows, replica statues and wall paintings imitating first century imitations of marble – a very amusing and colourful recreation whose wit is perhaps not intended. (The Trustees of the J. Paul Getty Museum).

pointing out its obvious functional appropriateness, and popularity, thinks it one of the most important buildings of the last ten years :

> As a functioning object, the Getty Museum appears to work as well as – or even better than – most recently built museums . . . [the designers] have evinced a far more sympathetic response to the needs of a popular audience than that expressed in any of the recently completed 'modern' image buildings which have been constructed in the U.S.[36]

Reyner Banham, known for his sometime celebration of such pop recreations, condemns the whole thing for its lifeless air, the 'bureaucratic precision' in detailing.

> The erudition and workmanship are as impeccable, and absolutely deathly, as this kind of pluperfect reconstruction must always be . . . no blood was spilled here, nor sperm, nor wine, nor other vital juice.

Basically, then, it isn't really Roman *enough* in its feeling and creation, the old charge of modernists that traditionalists tend in our century to give birth to the corpse. Charles Moore, otherwise sympathetic to this sort of thing, has also faulted it for lack of spatial invention.

My own impressions of this over-praised/over-condemned villa are somewhat different. It's exciting in its setting, certainly delightful to experience as a good replica (like Sir Arthur Evans' reconstructions at Knossus), very sympathetic to the antiquities displayed and even a challenge culturally, for it is saying that our time can indulge, like no other, in accurate historical simulation. Through our reproduction techniques (xerox, film, synthetic materials) and our specialised archaeologies (in this case archaeological and landscape specialists), with our high technologies of air-conditioning and temperature control and our structural capabilities (of putting the whole thing over a parking garage), we can do what nineteenth-century revivalists couldn't do. We can reproduce fragmented experiences of different cultures and, since all the media have been doing this for fifteen years, our sensibility has been modified. Thanks to colour magazines, travel and Kodak, Everyman has a well-stocked *musée imaginaire* and is a potential eclectic. At least he is exposed to a plurality of other cultures and he can make choices and discriminations from this wide corpus, whereas previous cultures were stuck with what they'd inherited.

Thus I would argue that the Getty Museum is a passable, if unintended, example of Post-Modern building, commendable for its pluralism and opening of choice but neither brilliant nor especially moribund. Perhaps the reason it has aroused a disproportionate amount of praise and blame is that it raised, at the right time, the question of what architecture should be in the seventies, but it didn't give the answers (so all sides were agitated).

Another similar event, Arthur Drexler's exhibition at the Museum of Modern Art entitled 'The Architecture of the Ecole des Beaux-Arts' (October 1975–January 1976) also posed the same question without giving a clear answer. Here was MOMA, the mother of the International Style in 1932, seeming to propose a return to nineteenth-century values : ornament instead of pseudo-functionalism (as Drexler would have it), urbanism and public buildings instead of mass housing, an attention to historical detail instead of an abstract, timeless statement. While the exhibition implied such alternatives, it was nevertheless indecisive about advocating a direct return to borrowing from Beaux-Arts building. One obvious problem was that this architecture had many of the faults of modernism : it was often as impersonal, heavy, and academic as the worst excesses of the International Style. More importantly, at the MOMA exhibition there was no theoretical context given for the use of the past, and without a coherent theory the show could only appeal to the sensibility, the new taste for the past – for 'roots' shall we say ?

In the same context there were many important books published on Victorian and Edwardian architecture in the early seventies, which implied an historicism without advocating it. Among those in English which contributed to the developing argument were Walter Kidney's *The*

Architecture of Choice: Eclecticism in America 1880–1930 (1974), *Edwardian Architecture and Its Origins*, edited by Alastair Service (1975), *Bay Area Houses,* edited by Sally Woodbridge (1976), *The Architecture of Victorian London,* by John Summerson (1976). These historians, especially younger ones such as John Beach, Gavin Stamp and Mark Girouard, are on the edge of influencing present practice, but their commitment has been mostly to the past as being over and done with. Still, if we are concerned with the growth of a post-modern tradition, their historical research is needed because they show the virtues of an eclectic architecture just before it was overpowered by Modernism. The examples of a rich vocabulary, that of 'Queen Anne Revival', that of Lutyens, were brought into the limelight to be studied by the current eclectics. 168 169

Neo-Vernacular

Another response to the obvious failure of Modern redevelopment and comprehensive renewal was a return to a 'kind of' vernacular. The inverted commas are necessary here (ersatz is the age of quotation marks) because the vernacular wasn't straight revivalist nor accurate reproduction, but 'quasi' or 'in the manner of' — a hybrid between modern and nineteenth-century brick building. The style, however, is highly recognisable and has the following attributes: nearly always pitched-roofs, chunky detailing, picturesque massing and brick, brick, brick. 'Brick is humanist', so the slogan goes (or gets caricatured), *so* humanist that you even find the ex-Brutalist Maekawa using it on skyscrapers in downtown Tokyo to bring back (I'm not kidding) 'humanity'. One understands why many Still-Modernists like James Stirling poke fun at 'The return of people's detailing in Noddy land'.[37] There is a kind of cosmetic thinness about much of this work, a folksy face disguising a grim, modern housing estate.

At any rate, ever since Jane Jacobs launched her attack on modern planning, there has been increasing demand for mixed renewal. This was in 1961, about the time Darbourne and Darke won the Pimlico competition in London against groups, such as Archigram, who favoured comprehensive rebuilding. The Darbourne and Darke solution nicely illustrates several of Jane Jacobs' points: it incorporates old buildings such as the dark brick nineteenth-century church; it mixes various activities, such as corner pubs, library, old age home and housing; it has a rich variety of spaces full of trees; and gives a definite sense of what every sixties architect was about — 'place'. Finally, it uses a 'Victorianesque' aesthetic of chunky brick and thus established, if not invented, the neo-vernacular style. 170

This style became in the seventies, for an impoverished and ideologically uncertain Britain, *the* style to fall back on when there were no other clear directions. It was or is acceptable to the majority of English people because it doesn't depart too far from the traditional family house (although Darbourne and Darke have added such 'un-English', modern elements as streets in the air, quasi-Mansarding and staccato, rather than individual house-by-house, massing.)

In an exhibition of work, from May–July 1977, Colin Amery and Lance Wright from the *Architectural Review* mark what they take to be the typical if understated mainstream of English architecture running from Pugin

168, 169 SIR EDWIN LUTYENS, 'Heathcote', Ilkley, Yorkshire, 1906. Lutyens' 'High Game' style uses the full repertoire of Doric elements — bases, columns, friezes, cornices — plus French refinements to produce a magnificent pile befitting a royal residence or Town Hall. The articulations and re-entrant angles make it an enjoyable game, as do the face metaphors of both wings. Lutyens is being reassessed today not only for his eclecticism, but also for his mastery of spatial contrast, and humour.

170 DARBOURNE and DARKE, *Pimlico Housing,* 1961–8, 67–70. The chunky brick aesthetic and volumes treated as giant decoration. This scheme mixed various uses in relatively low-rise high-density, and also mixed new and old building, landscapes, and masonry. The D&D projects always show a sensitivity to contrast which stems from the Picturesque Tradition. G. E. Street's Church of St James-the-Less has been preserved to become the focal point of the design. Brick was chosen partly for economic reasons, partly for associations which the inhabitants wanted : substantiality rather than 'flimsy-like panel construction'. (Brecht-Einzig Ltd.).

through Shaw, and Howard to the Letchworth Garden suburb.

> [It] restates particularly English virtues of domestic architecture. At the same time as many local authorities were indulging in an orgy of inhuman system building, Darbourne and Darke quietly proved that some of the essentials of domestic life like privacy, small gardens and good landscaping could be provided at high densities in cities within a framework of vernacular materials. . . Then there is the side so developed at Pershore – which is concerned with bringing back traditional (and therefore genial) materials and forms – a brick arch over the front door, windows that are more vertical in proportion . . .[38]

71

A more radical traditionalist like Jameson would, of course, show how many quirky neologisms Darbourne and Darke have introduced. Most seriously they have abolished the traditional street and created instead a large 'housing estate' – however fragmented in appearance. Thus this Neo-Vernacular was yet another half-way house, as the hyphenated appellation suggests, and not intended to be either modern or traditional, but a bit of both.

171 DARBOURNE and DARKE, *Pershore Housing,* 1976–7. Traditional English village architecture with pitched roofs, relieving arches, small passages and semi-private space. The window proportions and massing are atraditional, and some Purists have found the shapes ungainly, but the scheme represents a step towards the vernacular rather than an intention to arrive there. (Brecht-Einzig Ltd.).

172 MAGUIRE and MURRAY, *St John's College Staff Houses*, Bramcote, c. 1974. A picturesque version of rural stone architecture done in concrete block. These architects study the vernacular, partly the way Jameson does as a craft tradition, but their emphasis is here in manipulating this as a modest art form. Again the cost and inhabitants' response compare favourably with modernist schemes of a similar size.

Other English architects who worked in the method and style, again being acutely sensitive to scale and picturesque massing, were McGuire and Murray, Ahrends Burton and Koralek, Edward Cullinan, on occasion the GLC, and interior designer/architects such as Max Clendinning. So strong did the approach become that, by 1975, it could almost be proclaimed as official British policy (although policies such as these are never official, and certainly not proclaimed, in Britain). An indication is the Hillingdon Civic Centre, 1975–7, in its higgledy-piggledy Victorianesque of-course-brick, designed very much for and within the Welfare State by Andrew Derbyshire. He was explicit in justifying its intentions at the RIBA Conference.

172

173

> . . . we set out in this project to design . . . a building that spoke a language of form intelligible to its users (its occupants as well as the citizens of the borough) and used it to say something that they wanted to hear.[39]

There follows the grandiose claims that the building will

173 ANDREW DERBYSHIRE of ROBERT MATTHEW, JOHNSON, MARSHALL and PARTNERS, *Hillingdon Civic Centre*, 1974–7. Decorative brickwork around the windows, a large bureaucracy fragmented into a village scale, a collision of several pitched roofs

with Frank Lloyd Wright and 'human values'. The building is also curiously reminiscent of the large nineteenth century resort hotels in America. The architects consciously attempted to design within the users' language. (Sam Lambert, Architects' Journal).

break down administrative barriers and get everyone talking cordially with their elected representatives, as if the friendliness of the forms would suddenly induce a corresponding outbreak of hospitality in the neighbourhood. These claims, that architecture can radically change behaviour, are Modernist ones, although the attention to 'user-reactions' and actual social research are Post-Modern. Indeed the great emphasis on the *language* of architecture and the codes of the various groups who might use the building is precisely the Post-Modernism being advocated here. But the arguments are being applied with a kind of naive populism and literalism.

> Pitched roofs cover the steps of the wall section almost to ground level so that more roof — the protective, welcoming element — is seen than wall — the defensive, hostile element.[40]

One form equals one straightforward meaning is the implication. The whole notion of multiple readings, and readings which change over time, is reduced for the grand, popular meaning — pitched roofs = 'the protective, welcoming element'.

While it is impossible not to commend the new interest in actual, popular codes, the impression cannot be avoided that these are subtly being distorted and limited to good taste, middle-class versions of these codes. Indeed the work in the Neo-Vernacular sometimes suffers from a pervasive smugness, a kind of piety about being homespun that seeks to proclaim itself. This piety may be preferable to the deserts of mass-housing, with which this architecture is always contrasted, but it is somewhat less than a close reflection of existing architectural taste codes. Already the work of Venturi and Scott Brown had shown these to be richer than this 'Architect's Architecture' in brick.

The Neo-Vernacular made obvious and fitting connections with the trend towards rehabilitation and re-use that also became public policy by 1975 — this time it was proclaimed as European Architectural Heritage Year and a major approach of the GLC. A firm such as Feilden and Mawson could divide its time between restoration of historic monuments, straight modernism, and vernacular revival — such as their brick housing in Norwich designed on the model of the tall North European merchant's house. These designs not only went back to old prototypes, but also adopted ancient city patterns, existing street lines, and the wealth of accumulated accident — or rather the specific historic facts that made a street bend here, a row of houses twist and angle there. These quirky picturesque odd-spots, a delightful hallmark of the medieval city, finally became design formulae in the recent work of Aldo van Eyck and Théo Bosch.

Their scheme in Zwolle, built between 1975–7, renovates many buildings in the old historic centre and adds to these a mixed development: twenty-one businesses and seventy-five new houses. These, narrow and high like the traditional Dutch prototype, also conform to the existing, bending street pattern. Thus a series of spaces which are diverse: short alleys, small streets with arcades, streets with external staircases leading to residences on higher levels, semi-public space with gardens. The dwelling form truncates the gable roof — a typical Modernist decapitation showing the building is of Our Time — but otherwise extends traditional form in a marvellous way: for instance the interior spaces open through a veiled loggia, where one may look over the semi-public gardens, or up into sun-filled, distorted attic space. This rich ambiguity is

174, 175 FEILDEN and MAWSON, *Friars Quay Housing*, Norwich, 1972–5. Picturesque layout and the north European merchant's house adapted to this historical site near the Cathedral Close. The steep pitched roofs, variety of colour, and semi-private space add to feelings of historical continuity. Bernard Feilden has been involved with major restorations at St Paul's and York Cathedral.

176 ALDO VAN EYCK and THEO BOSCH, *Zwolle Housing*, 1975–7. Diverse functions and renovation combined with a new scheme based on the narrow Dutch facade — only the gable has been lopped off. The curving blocks are knitted into the traditional urban patterns to keep the street lines and neighbourhood identity. Sixteen types of residences were incorporated, many with semi-private gardens looking out on the public space.

177 *Zwolle*, view into loggia which acts as an intermediate space between living room, garden, and top floor.

178 VAN DEN BOUT and DE LEY, *Bickerseiland Housing*, Amsterdam, 1972–6. Narrow, deep houses with oriel windows, 'lightyards' in the centre, truncated gables (compare with the seventeenth century example) and semi-Brutalist detailing. Again a half-way house, or *neo*-Vernacular job, this cheap housing saved the area from being developed by outside commercial interests, much to the gratitude of the remaining community. An example, like Zwolle, of urban protest resulting in positive action.

Opposite
179 PETER EISENMAN, *House VI for the Franks*, Washington, Connecticut, 1975. The back side of the house continues the theme of a large flat plane placed frontally to the approach, and various lesser, vertical motifs placed at right angles to the direction of movement. Note the column lines marked on the outside either as extended pilaster, or wedge of space between two volumes. The front door is around to the left, the main bedroom is on the first floor to the right, above the living room. Find the hanging column in the middle if you can. (Norman McGrath). See page 109.

Inset
180 *Column and virtual stair.* The column is painted grey, or off-white to indicate different conditions — whether it carries a beam, electrical conduits, or nothing — and its relation to other planes. The false stair is painted red as opposed to the real, green stair (signifying stop and go?). (Charles Jencks).

characteristic of Post-Modern space, as we will argue later.

Van Eyck was called in on this project in 1970 in a typical protest of the time against inhumane city re-development. His arguments for renewal and infill housing can be taken as the toughest, unequivocal statement of a Modern architect just as he is becoming Post:

> What the snow image suggests in terms of the city is a careful adjustment, adaptation, modification and addition. Cities are chaotic and necessarily so. They are also kaleidoscopic. This should be accepted as a positive credo before it is too late . . . Add to this the notion that no abstract norm imposed from above, or any other motive, sanitary or speculative, can further justify the wanton destruction of existing buildings or street patterns . . . Ultimately, the world today can no longer afford such waste, nor can it afford to overlook the right of people to maintain both the built form as the social fabric of their domicile if that is their choice. Anything else is sociocide — local genocide with only the people left alive.[41]

Another project, which came out of the urban activism of the late sixties, was the Bickerseiland renewal in Amsterdam, where architects Van den Bout and De Ley also worked with the local community to provide infill, vernacular houses. Again these were tall, narrow and deep with a Dutch head flattened off just above the eyebrows, raising the question — if a Modernist could go this far backward, why couldn't he go the next step and get the remainder right?

It is interesting, in this context, to compare the Neo-Vernacular of different countries, let us say Joseph Esherick's Cannery in San Francisco and MBM's Santa Agueda in Benicassim, Spain — both worked on in the middle sixties. The former is a transformed nineteenth-century warehouse with modern graphics, and elevators shooting through, and enlivening, a tarted-up brick vernacular. Curves and arches are accentuated, the old fabric is heightened by reducing the window mullions to a minimum and using strong, contrasting colours. The result is very popular with the middle-class shopper, which is why such rehabilitations have been swiftly repeated from Australia to Canada. What they lose in terms of authenticity they gain in terms of jollity and it is probably

178

184

Opposite above
181 *Burns House*, exterior, in seventeen shades of earth colours, which create interesting recessions in depth. Moore develops the stucco-box tradition of Southern California, which Modernists such as Schindler had also exploited, for its economic and figurative potential. Any shape you want is relatively cheap. See page 126.

Opposite below left
182 CHARLES MOORE and ASSOCIATES, *Burns House*, Santa Monica Canyon, LA, 1974. The organ up the stairs give this view a rather religious overtone, but in the whole space it is set off against other strong elements such as a Mexican balcony (that acts as a small house to climb into). Light spills from various points, and back-lighting suggests a much greater depth than exists; the opposition of layered, skew space and monumental object is quite delightful. Moore can use traditional elements not only for their contrasts, but also in an easy-going, relaxed way.

Opposite below right
183 *Burns House* view up towards the private area, the attic-study to left, the bedroom and dressing rooms etc. to right. Handling various formal and functional elements at once — here books, stairs and cut-out screens — makes the space both mysterious and familiarly like an attic stair.

this quality that is both their economic saving and psychic curse.

The same is partly true of Martorell, Bohigas and Mac-Kay's traditionalesque housing with its picturesque 85 pantiles and inevitable brick. Like tourist resorts and Port Grimaud the aesthetic formula is really a class, and therefore an economic formula, because such comfortable and cosy images appeal to the middle class. In fact they cut across many social lines and appeal to the rich and poor in different countries. It would be false to term this a universal taste, or more popular than its opposite, Neo-Classical terrace housing, but it clearly articulates codes of meaning that go deep: friendliness conveyed through warm mixtures of wood and brick, individuality and ambiguity conveyed through broken massing, familiarity with respect conveyed by the choice of well-known elements. If it never quite lifts you off the ground with its brilliance or originality then it can be termed a success, because it was meant to be modest not heroic. In summarising this emergent strand of Post-Modernism at the RIBA Conference in 1976, I put together the following hodge-podge of a conclusion which tried to define what all the participants would agree is an unexceptional, common position.

> [Housing] should be small in scale, incorporate mixed uses and mixed ages of buildings, be rehabilitated where possible and put more on a craft than high art basis. It might be architect-designed, or based on pattern books modified to the particular situation. Wherever possible, it would be dweller controlled and sometimes it would be even self-built out of garbage and built in a pseudo-vernacular, depending on the taste of the culture for which it was built. Housing signifies a way of life . . .[42]

No other architect came closer to this goal (without reaching it) than Ralph Erskine.

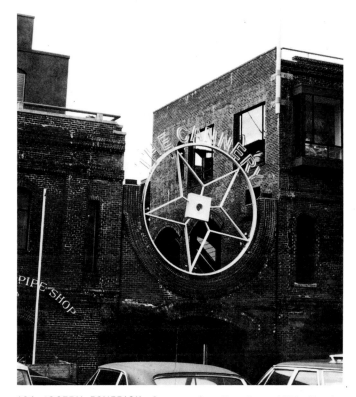

184 JOSEPH ESHERICK, *Cannery,* San Francisco, 1970. Nearly every historic city now has a converted area that has been somewhat pedestrianised to the great joy of shoppers. This middle classification of Victoriana (above all) robs it of guts, but supplies it with cash flow, a worthwhile, mephistophelian deal. Twee but alive, clean but rugged, phoney but authentic history, are the contradictory signs.

185 MARTORELL, BOHIGAS and MACKAY, *Santa Agueda,* Benicassim, Spain, 1966–7. A serious version of popular vernacular housing done in a picturesque way with pantiles and window blinds (that extend the living room space). MBM, exemplary eclectics, modify their style to suit the job; this is in one of their five current modes which also include the Industrial Style, Barcelona School Style, Pop Manner, and Eclectic Mode. (Xavier Miserachs).

Adhocism + Urbanist = Contextual

Erskine has designed in several styles, including the Neo-Vernacular which he used with consummate wit at Clare College, Cambridge, 1966. Here the small scale and domestic verge on the cloying and cutie-pie, but the whole thing is saved from mawkish charm by typical Erskinisms such as the cheapskate corrugated detailing and outrageous jokes — twelve feet of cantilevered doorway, cantilevered in brick, three inches from a support! Erskine has turned the expedient and *ad hoc* into a kind of art form, where his own happy-go-lucky style is clearly recognisable. At Byker, outside Newcastle, he has built a community of housing which will probably rank with the Weissenhof Settlement, Stuttgart, 1927, in establishing the paradigm to follow.

First among its principles and most importantly, the Byker community has a degree of self-government, a certain local power to balance that of the central city. To support this, the architect set up his office on the building site and allowed the people being rehoused (9,500) to choose their location, friends and apartment plan (within a restricted budget). This participation in the planning process helped form and continue the community, as much as did the preservation of the existing social ties. Since eighty per cent of the people remained within the area during the building, most of the old associations remained too.

Indeed several important buildings were preserved, churches, a gymnasium and local buildings, so that the resultant patch-work has a depth of historical association much greater than the typical modernist new town. Classical elements, discarded building parts, ornament from previous buildings were incorporated either as decoration or use — such as seats and tables transformed *ad hoc* from column capitals.

In the Byker renewal, Erskine allowed the multi-use of activities and corresponding multi-expression of function, although it must be admitted this articulation is more in his own *ad hoc* style than in the local codes of Byker. Every house, and seventy per cent are on ground level, has a private domain and is surrounded by semi-private space such as gardens and small walkways. Even the exterior apartment corridors in the Byker 'wall' are broken up and given local planting, so that this large block has the identity and safety so lacking in the old paradigm, Pruitt-Igoe and other famous monsters of Modernism.

Erskine shows that, in the words of John Turner, architecture really is a verb, an *action* not just a set of correct theories or prescriptions. His office became immersed in the Byker community by setting up shop in a disused funeral parlour, selling plants and flowers (an obvious popular activity in England), acting as the local 'lost and found', that is, doing countless non-architectural things as he got to know the people, and they his team. Then the slow process of design and construction took place, endless discussions and rather small decisions, so that landscape, 'doorway', colour, history, idiosyncrasy and other non-commensurables could find a place. The success of the result, both as an amusing and humane environment make this a key Post-Modern project in theory, if not in precise coding (there might have been more, traditional houses and renewal). But the success depends to a large part on Erskine's inimitable free-wheeling openness which could, without intimidation, gain the confidence of the people and allow the process to happen

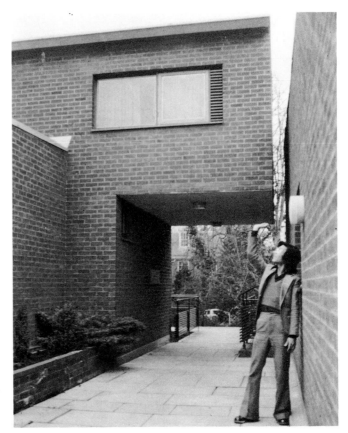

186 RALPH ERSKINE, *Clare College*, Cambridge, 1972, entrance showing brick cantilevered almost to a support, but then saved in time — all doors should have *something* odd about them.

187 RALPH ERSKINE, *Byker Architects' Office*, Newcastle, 1972–4, in a converted funeral parlour. The red, white and blue graphics rise as optimistically as the balloon on this office in the heart of the renewal. The designers were accessible to the inhabitants who had a say in their future location, neighbours, and type of apartment.

— the verb to conjugate. How one generalises or teaches this art, apart from example, remains a mystery.

It does seem, however, that the pluralist language of Byker results partly from the participatory process. 'Participation in design' became in Britain during the seventies a respectable if loaded term which usually meant a one-sided consultation with those being designed for: they could see the plans beforehand, but didn't have the expertise or power to propose viable alternatives.[43] At Louvain University, Lucien Kroll and

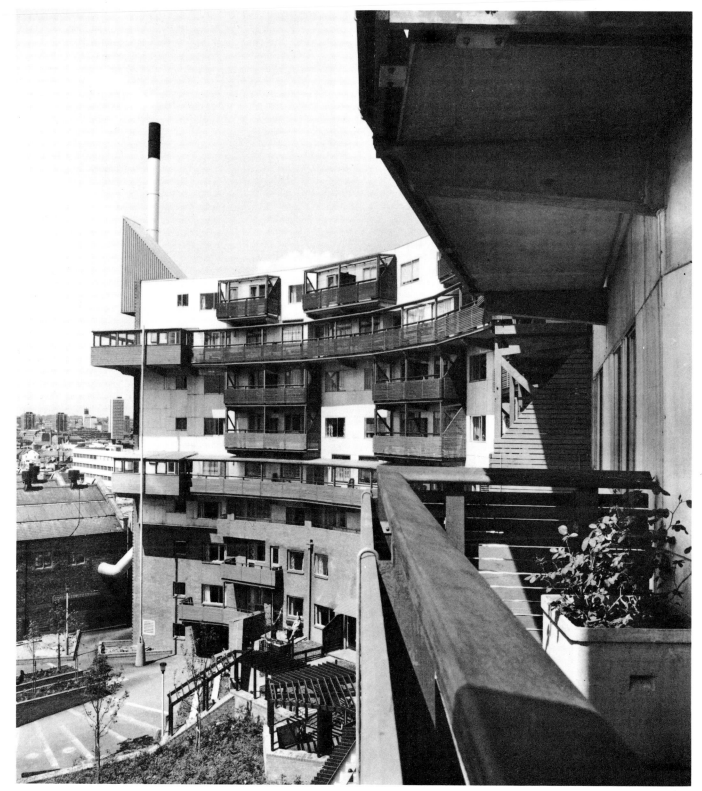

188 RALPH ERSKINE, *Byker Wall,* Newcastle, 1974. A mixture of materials used in a semantic way : brick in the lower two floors, corrugated metal and asbestos in the upper ones ; semi-private deck in green stained wood, circulation in blue, and untamed nature at the base. These articulations break down a potentially massive wall, and give it a human scale. (Bill Toomey, Architectural Press).

189 his team took the process further and really involved a community (or part of it) in design decisions.

The students, who were divided into flexible teams, participated in designing the buildings along with Kroll, who acted rather like an orchestra leader. They shifted small bits of plastic foam around in working out the overall model. When disputes arose, or one group became too dogmatic and fixed, Kroll reorganised the teams so that each one became familiar with each other's problems, until a possible solution was in sight. Not until then did he draw up the plans and sections which made it workable. The resultant buildings show a complexity and richness of meaning, a delicate pluralism, that usually takes years to achieve and is the result of many inhabitants making

189 LUCIEN KROLL and ATELIER, *Medical Faculty Buildings*, University of Louvain, near Brussels, 1969–74. An artificial hill town of various activities, articulated with different building systems. The large glazed area is communal, also the restaurant space; the other material – wood, brick, plastic, aluminium and concrete – are also used semantically. Traditional signs are incorporated: greenhouses, pitched roof and chimneys signify the more private areas. The variety and detail simulate the piecemeal decisions which take place over time and give identity to any old city.

190 View across the main Piazza showing builders' contribution to design. The rocks grow up from the ground into brick and then tile. Participation and individualism have produced a witty environment, which only lacks normality. One longs for a bit of straight Modernism here or even Aldo Rossi.

190 small adjustments over time.

The variety of codes and uses in the buildings clearly reflect the fact that opposite values are being realised, but even here there are biases in the result. The aesthetic is everywhere picturesque, as if normality and the silent majority have been rigorously snubbed.

By following only one mode of interaction in design, Kroll has actually precluded everyday, impersonal architecture, and thus one longs here for a judicious bit of the International Style. Post-Modernism accepts Modernism not only for factories and hospitals, but also for semiotic balance, for its place within a system of meaning. As soon as the system swings too far towards the idiosyncratic and
191 *ad hoc*, it invites the return of the Neo-Classical, even 'Fascist Style', not for the 'rational' justifications which its adherents may proffer, but for reasons of signification and richness.[44] Meaning consists in oppositions within a system, a dialectic in space or over time.

The politically motivated group in Brussels, ARAU, have used these oppositions for their own ends: stopping
192 large-scale redevelopment in the capital of the Common Market. Basically they use pastiche, Port Grimaud and

true Brussels vernacular in opposition to the Modernism proposed by ITT and other multinationals. When the multinational comes with its scheme for a disruptive high-rise, ARAU (*Atelier de Recherche et d'Action Urbaine*) meet it with a counter-proposal. This action group organises neighbourhood support, calls a press conference, agitates through the newspapers and uses its *counter-design* to stop or redirect the original proposal. ARAU has successfully fought a dozen or more such battles, using attractive pastiche as an urban weapon, and it's interesting to note that this style, or several modes, come about through the participatory activity. Maurice Culot, one of its members, has said:

> For ARAU members the city is a place where democracy could live – they reject any proposal that banishes inhabitants from the city . . . My mission is not to create new forms but only to explain the options and programmes being debated by ARAU. We do not force our own architectural tastes on people, but follow the advice of the people involved.[45]

The next step could be a form of architectural larceny: ARAU might appropriate the commission from the

192 ARAU, *Brussels,* 1975. This group uses various counter-designs to stop massive redevelopment, leaving it up to the community to choose which alternative, or combination, they want. Using pastiche, Port Grimaud, or here Honfleur and Van Eyck as alternatives to modernist redevelopment, they seek to confirm the underlying city patterns.

191 BRUCE GOFF, *Bavinger House,* Norman, Oklahoma, 1957. Goff is the master of *ad hoc* building, or the 'Army and Navy Surplus Aesthetic', using any conceivable left-over materials. Here a continuous spiral of space is surrounded by sandstone and rubble picked up on the site. A mast and steel cables lifted from boat technology hold up the roof. But he also uses natural, organic materials, such as the untreated, wooden mullions, cut from nearby trees. In addition to all this Goff is the only major architect who uses schlock in a convincing way. He forces us to re-examine taste-cultures which have heretofore been disregarded.

193 NIEUMARKET *protest in Amsterdam,* 1975, to protest constant demolition of the old quarters for a new metro. Continual battles have led to some buildings and areas being saved, but the slaughter can be read as 'handwriting on the wall' (inside the ghost image of the destroyed buildings) : 'loss of apartments through war 366, 10 years of renewal 335, from the metro 115, new buildings 1946–74 6 apartments'. The Amsterdamers never tire of finding new ways of announcing their plight.

original designers and actually build their counter-design – then neighbourhood participation would begin to mean something.

While it's unlikely that such illegalities would be supported by Shell, Ford and the World Trade Center, it's also wrong to assume that this activism is entirely barren. Aside from changing the climate of opinion (and multi-nationals are now themselves adopting a form of local pastiche), such protests have stopped destruction in many large cities – for instance in the Covent Garden area in London and the Nieumarket in Amsterdam. Advocacy planning in America was also effective in stopping urban disruption, although it too couldn't initiate development. At Zwolle, as we have seen, the community finally acted positively after it was threatened by redevelopment, and the same is true at Byker in a somewhat different context. Maurice Culot's relative success is suggestive, I think, not only for its use of various styles and counter-schemes, but also because it stems from an institutional base. ARAU is formalised, it has links with lawyers and other professionals, and can work with the hundred or so already existing action committees in Brussels. If these

neighbourhood groups can become stronger, as strong as their suburbanite counterparts, then the long history of indiscriminate city destruction may be reversed.

The Modern Movement has played a role in the deterioration of cities by supporting new towns, disurbanisation and comprehensive redevelopment – all anti-city trends – but apologists would claim that really the villain at large is consumer society, the motorcar and the pull of suburbia. Whoever is finally convicted of the crime, it's clear that the Modern Movement did nothing much to solve it. They

194 LEO KRIER, *Royal Mint Square Housing*, project, 1974. The traditional street lines and block are saved, but the site is bisected by a 'public room' with various ceremonial and functional elements (including kiosks and entrance portico). Several old houses are retained as well; the scheme only suffers from a slight case of pomp and monotony.

195 LEO KRIER, *Echternach project*, 1970. The tourist map view of this Luxembourgeois city stitches together medieval, Baroque and modern elements. Circuses, grand avenues, and endless bay repetition reminiscent of Bath or Haussmann. Every city, Krier seems to be saying, should have its urbanist-eye-view kept in order so that the public parts – squares, streets, monuments – articulate its memory.

had no great political and social theory of how a city thrives and how civic virtues are cultivated and nurtured.

The Post-Modernists, Culot, the Krier brothers, Conrad Jameson for instance, take a different view of city life and stress the active, valuative aspect. The planner, architect or market researcher *intervenes* to bring about those values he supports, but he does this within a democratic, political context where his values can be made explicit and debated. The proper place for much that now happens as architecture or planning, Jameson contends, is the political forum – the neighbourhood meeting or the meeting of political representatives. While no adequate city forum exists to express or guarantee this process, Post-Modernists insist on its desirability.

Basically this is a return to an old and never perfect institution, the public realm – the agora, the assembly area, mosque or gymnasium that acted as a space for people to debate their varying views of the good life or assert their communalty.[46] While it would be premature to claim a unanimity of views on this, the public realm comes back as the major focus of design in the schemes of the Rationalists, Charles Moore, Ricardo Bofill, Antoine Grumbach and the Krier brothers. Only Robert Venturi among the Post-Modernists takes a stand against the agora and *palazzo pubblico*, and he does this, as we have seen, for communicational and not political reasons.

194 Robert and Leo Krier in particular have celebrated the public realm in many of their design schemes and competition entries. They have also mounted well-observed attacks on the devastation of city fabric. They criticise all the forces, whether economic, ideological or modernistic, which have destroyed the texture of cities, and then propose elegant alternatives to patch it up, or to create new wholes.

Basically the Krier brothers follow Camillo Sitte's notion of articulating continuous urban space as a negative volume that flows and pulsates and reaches a crescendo around public buildings – a cathedral or school may serve as the pretext for the agora. This patching of urban, public space is the antithesis of Modernistic practice – the free standing, functionalist monument.

195 In the Echternach project, Leo Krier inserts a traditional arcade and circus, using the existing morphology of the eighteenth century to create an identifiable spine to the town and a culmination of the entrance route at the existing abbey. Height, scale, silhouette, building materials are all compatible with the existing fabric, although accentuated to give a new emphasis to the public realm. Leo Krier uses the traditional aerial perspective of tourist maps to stitch these forms together, and a master-planning concept whose grand sweep is reminiscent of Bath. Such historicist methods are combined with a Corbusian language of form resulting in that characteristic schizophrenia of expression about which the reader must now be tired of hearing.

196 In his entry for the La Villette Competition Krier has proposed a return to the intimate scale of historic cities by creating a unit urban block based on a collectivity of twelve or so families. These closely-grained blocks are then used as a background fabric against which the more public buildings stand out along a centre spine. The idea is a return to the historic city of Paris, and to an architectural language based on socially recognisable types.

> These large buildings crystallise Types of buildings like The Theatre, The Library, The Hotel, into specific architectural models. They are not to be understood as unique signs – as words in an esoteric language – but rather as an attempt to create a system of social and formal references which would make up the landmarks of a contemporary city, replacing the traditional religious and institutional landmarks with building Types of a new social content.[47]

197 The 'new social content', inevitably Marxist for Krier, is as Modernist as his Rationalist language of Types, and the latter is not bound to communicate socially, as intended, 198

1. Bird's-eye-view of Quartier de la Villette at 300 m altitude.

196 LEO KRIER, *La Villette Competition*, Paris, 2nd prize, 1976. Made up of small, community units of almost a dozen or so families which, Krier contends, would have local control, this scheme nevertheless has a grand, centralised imagery (all the housing looks the same). A grand public boulevard runs north/south (right/left) containing the Place Centrale, Place de la Mairie, and Square des Congrès. Rolling English parks create the other axis which focuses on historic Paris. The biplanes are also reminiscent of Le Corbusier.

197, 198 LEO KRIER, *La Villette typology*, of the Hotel and Cultural Centre. The ziggurat is lifted from its historical context, and Ledoux's design for a barn is turned into a town hall cut into four parts. Krier's hope for a universal language that could be understood founders on the same misunderstandings that plagued Ledoux and Le Corbusier.

The meaning of form is social and temporal, and cannot be established by fiat, especially based on abstractions. It is curious that Krier, who attacks Le Corbusier for his urban insensitivity, should have such similar notions, but the theory of how architecture communicates is not widely understood.

199 GIAMBATTISTA NOLLI, *Map of Rome*, 1748. Private building in grey cross-hatching is hollowed out by public space in white, which may be either street, piazza, courtyard or church interior. The map gives a nice idea of semi-public space and the way it mediates between the major antimony, public and private.

200 HADRIAN'S VILLA, Tivoli, AD 118–134. A series of axially oriented set-pieces brought from all parts of the Roman world in this early eclectic complex: temples and canals were copied from Egypt, caryatids from Greece, and there was even a place for 'Hades' here. The most exquisite part of this villa retreat (it is really a small town) is the *Teatro Marittime* (middle left) with its circular canals and complex overlap of exedra, convex and concave. Here Hadrian retired to his 'library' to read, eat, and bathe. Colin Rowe has said 'The Villa Adriana presents the demands of the ideal and recognises at the same time the needs of the *ad hoc*'.

because of its abstract, atemporal character. Nonetheless the intentions of establishing a language, a public symbolism, and knitting this within the fabric of Paris are exemplary. Furthermore, Krier sees this city building as gaining its meaning from various dialectics – that between the private and public realm, the present and the past and the morphology of solid and void. This semiotic intention and city of dialectical meaning takes us to the writings of Colin Rowe and the practice known as Contextualism.

As a philosophy and movement, Contextualism started in the early sixties at Cornell University with studies into the way cities formed various binary patterns which give legibility. Alvin Boyarsky looked at Camillo Sitte's work for its implications, just as George Collins was doing at the time, and the most important binary pair emerged from Sitte's drawings: the opposition between solid and void, or figure and ground. As Grahame Shane describes the language of Contextualism, with its inevitable abstract dualities (as if the theorists had all been trained by Heinrich Wollflin, with two slide projectors) there are

urban patterns of *regular* vs *irregular*, *formal* vs *informal*, *types* vs *variants*, *figures* vs *fields* (if effectively combined known as *set-pieces*), *centre* vs *infill*, *tissue* vs *boundary edge* and ho vs hum.

Such a glossary could begin with the term *context*. By definition the design must fit with, respond to, mediate its surroundings, perhaps completing a pattern implicit in the street layout or introducing a new one. Crucial to this appreciation of urban patterns is the Gestalt double image of the *figure-ground*. This pattern, which can be read either way – solid or void, black or white – is the key to the contextualist approach to urban space.[48]

According to this argument, the failure of modern architecture and planning, very briefly, was its lack of understanding the urban context, its over-emphasis on objects rather than the tissue between them, design from the inside-out rather than the exterior space to the inside. By pondering hard on the large chunks of blackened areas in Sitte's drawings, and at Nolli's seventeenth-century map

199

201 O. M. UNGERS et al, *Student Hostel Competition*, 1963. Like Hadrian's Villa, a series of set-pieces are repeated and organised on their own axis which cross and sometimes collide. Multiple geometries, dissonant angles, and a subtle public order.

of Rome, the Contextualists found, as did Robert Venturi, a new respect for *'poché'* or left-over, tissue building – the 'ground' for any city's attractive 'figures'.

To Colin Rowe and his Gibbonian prose fell the job of weaving all these dualities into a spellbinding dialectic of binary pairs, which recommended itself perhaps more as suggestive analogy than as precise prescription. His 'Collage City' set up arguments between the mechanism of Enlightenment thinkers and the organicism of the Hegelians, the olde worlde fantasies of the Americans without roots at Disneyland, and the Brave New World of Superstudio with too much past in Florence. He contrasted the fixed, Platonic utopias of the Renaissance with the 'utopia as extrusion' of the Futurists, the single, big ideas of the 'hedgehogs' and the many, little goals of the 'foxes'.

> Palladio is a hedgehog, Giulio Romano, a fox; Hawksmoor, Soane, Philip Webb are probably hedgehogs, Wren, Nash, Norman Shaw almost certainly foxes . . .[49]

Such games and analogical thinking work most effectively when Rowe uses one side of his equation to criticise the other and comes up with a compound which includes both antinomies. Thus his 'collage city', based on the *bricolage* of many different utopias (or the 'vest pocket utopias – Swiss Canton, New England village, Dome of the Rock, Place Vendôme' etc) has everything both ways with a beneficent vengeance: 'the enjoyment of utopian poetics without our being obliged to suffer the embarrassment of utopian politics'.

The buildings of Hadrian, his pluralist Pantheon, his Rome, especially his villa at Tivoli are *ad hoc* compilations and dialectical utopias. In fact during the sixties Hadrian's villa becomes *the* exemplar, a model and point of reference for such various architects and critics as Louis Kahn and Siegfried Giedion, Mathias Ungers and Vincent Scully – in short Modernists and Post-Modernists. For some it is the richness of overlapping spatial focii which is the lesson of the villa, for others the eclecticism of sources (Egypt and Greece), the palimpsest of meaning or the mannerism of sharp juxtaposition. For Rowe it is the supreme instance of fox-like dialectic.

> For if Versailles may be a sketch for total design in a context of total politics, the Villa Adriana attempts to dissimulate all reference to any single controlling idea . . . Hadrian, who proposes the reverse of any 'totality', seems only to need accumulation of the most various fragments . . . The Villa Adriana is a miniature Rome. It plausibly reproduces all the collisions of set pieces and all the random empirical happenings which the city so lavishly exhibited . . . It is almost certain that the uninhibited aesthetic preference of today is for the structural discontinuities and the multiple syncopated excitements which the Villa Adriana presents . . . the bias of this [anti-hedgehog] argument should be clear: it is better to think of an aggregation of small, and even contradictory set pieces (almost like the products of different régimes) than to entertain fantasies about total and 'faultless' solutions which the condition of politics can only abort.[50]

This argument for Collision City was, like that of *Adhocism* based on the method of *bricolage* and the importance of memory in forming a base for prophecy and city design.[51] It mustered the examples of several semi-historicists mentioned here at the outset – Lubetkin, Luigi Moretti – who juxtaposed past with present to gain a richer meaning. I mention these common points of interest not to prove any priority of influence, but rather to show an emergent consensus in some quarters, a consensus which is perhaps best represented by the Dusseldorf scheme of James Stirling. Because here by 1975 we have a leading *modern* architect using *bricolage* as a technique to knit and sometimes jam the past and the present together, and mediate between that basic antinomy: the solid urban tissues and the void of public realm. Stirling uses a wrap-around nineteenth-century facade on one side to fit into the context, and crumbles it away on the other side, thus indicating a knowing pastiche. He pulls a pedestrian route from the more dense urban fabric into a circular court and then inverts this, dialectically, into a square object (the ground has become figure, the circle squared). This pronounced object is then inflected on its podium to acknowledge a major city axis and act as a focusing monument – becoming thereby one more in a neighbour-

202, 203 JAMES STIRLING, *Dusseldorf Museum Project*, 1975. A sensitive example of contextual infill, where the height, scale and masonry of the area are respected, but the symbolic elements are still allowed their expression. The entrance cube inflects from the grid and is also a major focus for site lines which relate to other monuments. The nineteenth century facade to the left is wrapped around part of the new museum. Glass sheeting, the only Modernist remnant, is appropriately used in a semantic way as public circulation and congregation area. (John Donat).

hood group. Except for esoteric references to Schinkel and Albert Speer, and the reticence in historical detailing (blank pediment, no pilasters) this project represents a new stage in Post-Modern urbanism, because it shows a modern architect acting with the kind of sensitivity towards the historical context one would expect of a traditionalist, with the freshness and invention of a Renaissance architect.

Metaphor and Metaphysics

Another motive causing architects to leave the tenets of Modernism was its obvious inability to deal with or pose general questions of architectural meaning: what was architecture 'to be about', especially now that the Modernist beliefs in progressivist technology and the Machine Aesthetic were seen to be so naive (or boring)? Architecture must have a signifying reference – the Renaissance had its Platonic metaphysics, the Romans their belief in Imperial organisation – what is ours to reflect, beyond a polite agnosticism?

One of the particularly defining characteristics of Post-Modernism is its pursuit of odd metaphysics, 'after strange gods' as it were, instead of the familiar and tired gods of process and pragmatism.[52] But even with the machine metaphor dead, our age is not much closer to credible metaphors or a developed metaphysics. Science, in its agnosticism, can hardly provide the answers – although it can refute them. Furthermore, any metaphysics is thrown into question today for two quite different reasons: it is often too idiosyncratic to capture the imagination of society at large, and it doesn't build up a foundation in habit and ritual, since industrial society tends to erode or commercialise this traditional base.

Nonetheless the spiritual function of architecture remains, in fact will not go away even if a religion and metaphysics are lacking, and thus the Post-Modern architect like the Surrealist painter, crystallises his own spiritual realm around the possible metaphors at hand. The metaphysics are then expressed as either implicit or explicit metaphor which is signified in the form. Perhaps the earlier argument (pages 40–52) should be summarised. The most renowned metaphorical buildings – Ronchamp, the Sydney Opera House, TWA – vary in their coding from implicit to explicit, from mixed metaphor to congruent simile. An architectural 'simile' is, as in writing or speech, the formal and explicit statement of a metaphor -- the hot dog stand that has so many other cues such as mustard and bun that one can say it is explicitly intended.

On the other hand most architectural metaphors are implicit and mixed. The overriding metaphor which recent architects have just started to express grows out of the organic tradition of modernism and relates very closely to body images and man's continuity with the natural and animal kingdoms. We can see a metaphysics in its primitive stage now making use of very direct similes. The human body, the face, the symmetry of animal forms are becoming the foundation for a metaphysics that man finds immediate and relevant. Beyond this, he responds willingly and unconsciously to body images, the haptic metaphors of inside and out, up and down, projections of his own internal body orientation. Even his description of architecture is coloured by this imagery. Buildings 'lie on the horizon', or 'rise up from it', have 'a front' which is more acceptable than 'a back' (just like living beings) and are 'dressed up' or 'plain'.

Charles Moore and Kent Bloomer who have analysed these body images in relation to architecture claim they form a basic model for the experience of the environment, and one not limited to the priority of sight.

> By combining the values and feelings that we assign to internal landmarks with the moral qualities that we impart to psycho-physical coordinates, [right/left etc] we can imagine a model of exceptionally rich and sensitive body meanings. It is a comprehensible model (because we 'possess' it), although it is much more humanely complex than a mathematical matrix.[53]

For such reasons the city, just as the home, is considered empty without its anthropomorphic dimensions, its central 'heart' or equivalent to the main piazza, the symbolic focus.

The house has so many such anthropomorphic focii that it may be considered a living proof of the validity of the 'pathetic fallacy'. We project not only a heart (hearth) but, as Carl Jung has pointed out the whole anatomy of the face and body.[54] In his example, an eighteenth-century

204 MAISON DES CARIATIDES, *28 rue Chaudronnerie*, Dijon, c. 1610. Something like thirty-seven heads decorate this house, perhaps too many even for a Mannerist. The mixing of architectural and human members is quite extraordinary in its ingenuity; note for instance the careful asymmetries set against the ordered use of pilaster-people. Windows, doors, chimneys and other places of transition or focus were celebrated with complex metaphors, quite appropriate for the erogenous zones of architecture.

Hebrew text, the turrets of the house are the ears, the furnace is the stomach and the windows, as usual, eyes. The house is, as mentioned above (pages 54–5) often perceived as a face, and found decapitated when given a flat roof.

During the Renaissance such body images were conventionalised and incorporated into architectural dimensions. The human body was inscribed both into the plan and elevation of churches, and the metaphor was taken so seriously that Bernini was even criticised because his piazza for St Peter's resulted in a contorted figure with mangled arms.[55] Any doubt that man is obsessed by an architecture in his own image, or at least his own image projected onto architectural facades, can be dispelled by counting the caryatids, herms, terms and so forth that are peppered throughout any large European city, a veritable menagerie of funny faces and strange races.

Recently, Post-Modern architects have taken up the anthropomorphic metaphor and metaphysics in a direct and sometimes vulgar way turning the image into an explicit simile. Thus Minoru Takeyama's Beverly Tom Hotel, 1974, is in the shape of the Shinto 'tenri' symbol, that is to say a phallus – a symbol repeated throughout the hotel in the details, down to the ashtrays! What

204

206

205 STANLEY TIGERMAN, *Hot Dog House*, North Western Illinois, 1975–6. A simple 14 x 70 foot vacation house built for $35 000; blank, dumb cedar wall on the entrance side and glass-wall-Mondrian on the viewing side. The private, weekend house in the country has always afforded opportunity for visual puns, and hot dog is just one possible metaphor here. Torso and ampule are coded as well. (Philip Turner).

metaphysics justifies such metaphor? It is clear that the vertical shape may have led to the symbol, and hotels are in a banal sense corridors of power, but neither rationalisation can sufficiently explain the phallus, which seems to be the abstract statement of primitive power in the industrial landscape. But then again why *this* hotel as a phallus? It's not the equivalent of a dolmen, Place Vendôme, obelisk, or Christian spire — the building task can't carry here such strong content.

Stanley Tigerman also uses explicit metaphors to generate architecture: the 'Animal Cracker House', Hot 205 Dog House, Zipper apartments and again a phallus-shaped building called euphemistically 'the Daisy House'. Here the justification came from the client, who had seen the Hot Dog House and wanted something visually edible too. Various lubricious reasons led to the final form, 207 perhaps the most printable being that Tigerman wanted 208 to make his client laugh. At any rate, the significance for us is not so much whether Tigerman's or Takeyama's similes are ultimately justifiable and profound but rather that, unlike Modern architects, they have felt a need to use the metaphorical plane of expression. The results may be raw and occasionally ludicrous, but the architect has *intended* to use this mode of speech, recently confined to the commercial sector with its giant donuts and hot dogs, and his buildings thus are not the misfired metaphors of Malapropistic Modernism, but the overfired metaphors of Post-Modernism in its first stage.

Possibly because metaphor and symbolism were suppressed by the modern movement their re-emergence now

206 MINORU TAKEYAMA, *Hotel Beverly Tom*, Hokkaido, 1973–4. Eighty rooms in this hotel are syncopated in three quarters of the cylinder; a restaurant and roof garden are indicated by the other syntactic changes. The overall phallic form is not absolutely legible — this symbolism is coded with other, functional meanings.

207, 208 STANLEY TIGERMAN, *Daisy House*, Indiana, 1976–7. The plan and parts of the elevation mapped with varying degrees of subtlety to well known parts of the male and female anatomy. These shapes, partly due to the client's wishes, are again finished off with a series of oppositions — the flat stucco wall versus textured cedar curves, rectilinear window grid versus curvilinear viewing panes. One blank side is for public entrance and kitchen, the other flat side for viewing the lake. This elevation is a transformation of the plan which visually implies that the phallus continues forward onto the deck and that the windows go on into the ground. The symbolic arched entrance presently lacks its Spanish Mission bell.

at a time of unsettled metaphysics is bound to be over-emphatic; but Post-Modernists are nonetheless committed to exploring this level of meaning.

One of the most pervasive, implied metaphors in house building has been the suggested image of the face. Children often draw their home as a face, and we project, empathetically, our feelings and dimensions onto buildings. Other anthropomorphic parts have been represented in traditional architecture — a balance of supports suggesting legs, a bodily symmetry, a proportion suggesting human ratios of arm to torso — which have given it a familiarity and welcome disposition. The row houses of Amsterdam with their high, pitched gables, symmetrical visage and face-like orifices, stare out at you like so many prosperous and individualistic burghers in a guild portrait by Rembrandt. This metaphor, a commonplace for centuries, is coded in such a way that the contradiction between competition and civic pride is directly portrayed: each is given equal weight in these 'cheek by jowl' facades. Furthermore the coding is mixed and ambiguous unlike, say, the face buildings of the Italian Renaissance — the Zuccaro Palace in Rome, and the faces at Bomarzo. These latter so overcode the forms that the face no longer welcomes but alienates, or mystifies.

The Japanese architect Kazumasu Yamashita has taken this strand of tradition to its logically absurd conclusion

209 *Gable watching in Amsterdam* is an enjoyable pastime since the faces of these buildings are as different and engaging as those seen in typical portraits of Dutch burghers. Animals as well as the face and body are also literally present in the decoration.

209

210

210 FEDERIGO ZUCCARO, *Palazzo facade Via Gregoriana,* Rome, c. 1592. The traditional metaphor of windows as the eyes of a building is here dislocated to the mouth. The doorway grimaces while the windows smile. Note the way pediments, keystones and cornucopia intersect the face. The flaring nostrils and general physiognomy are similar to that at Bomarzo. Is this the conventional entrance to Hades?

in Kyoto. Here his Face House, with its round eyes and gun-barrel nose, scowls and yells and ultimately swallows the inhabitant. By mapping the forms so literally the metaphor becomes reductive — 'this is nothing but an inscrutable face'. This reductivism, always a danger of simile, should be contrasted with the Amsterdam examples or the popular bungalows in America with their multi-projecting foreheads, or the anthropomorphic creations of Bernard Maybeck. 21

Maybeck's houses often mix architectural and non-architectural metaphors, codes inside the professional elite with popular codes. For this inclusive eclecticism he, along with Lutyens and Gaudí, has become another Pre-Modernist for study. His Roos House, 1909, suggests metaphors concerning Tudor and Gothic periods as well as the actual location in the Bay Area of San Francisco, but these are subtly blended with a wide-faced visage. The forehead is perhaps more a broken eave-line; the eyes recall first Gothic trefoils and *œil de bœuf* before they invite us to find the lens and iris; the balcony is an exuberant version of *Flamboyante* before it is a mouth. So the face image, which definitely looms out at us once we see it, still can retreat into its former context and remain background. 139

I have attempted a similar mixed coding in a studio building, the profile is the normal Cape Cod pitched-roof, the mouth, teeth and eyebrows are more purely 21

211 KAZUMASA YAMASHITA, *Face House,* Kyoto, 1974. You are swallowed by a scowl, the eyes bulge out and the nose needs plastic surgery. Such literalism suggests these unsympathetic remarks and the question — 'ah, but where are the ears?' Either less or more explicit coding should have been attempted. (Ryuji Miyamoto).

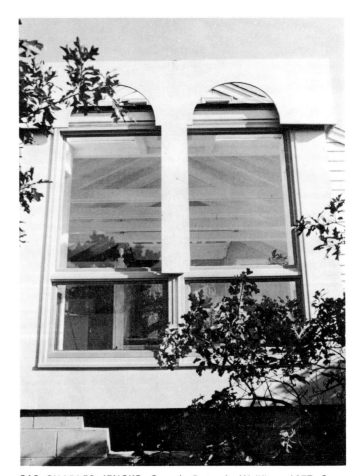

212 CHARLES JENCKS, *Garagia Rotunda,* Wellfleet, 1977. Symmetrical ends of pitched buildings often produce a physiognomic expression quite by chance. Here the face is partly in purdah, with the teeth basement hidden by shrubbery. The eyes and nose are painted blue on the inside face to give a reflected light and contrast with the sky. The metaphor is somewhat veiled as a geometric pattern of arches and verticals.

213 MICHAEL GRAVES, *Claghorn House,* Princeton, 1974. Lattice work, string courses, a broken pediment and sign of pitched roof (parapet slant) are just recognisable in this addition to a Queen Anne house. The architectural elements take on natural metaphors (brown, earth base, green for shrubbery, blue framing for sky). The cruciform post and beam frames the sky and acts as a gate proportioned to human dimensions. (Carol Constant).

214 ANTONIO GAUDI, *Casa Batllo,* facade, 1904–6. A masterful use of metaphor with a metaphysical base. Bones and lava articulate the bottom two floors given over to shops and the main apartment. Death masks and the undulating sea metaphor articulate similar apartments in the middle, while a sleepy dragon looks down from the roof. The building represents Barcelona's separatist hopes: her Patron Saint, St. George, kills the dragon of Spain who has eaten up the Catalan people – the bones and skeletons remain as monuments to the martyrs. (Esquela Technica Superior de Arquitectura de Barcelona).

architectural in their suggestion and even the explicit eyes and nose are here familiar enough architectural elements to seem merely arches and plane. The face is then perhaps not immediately recognisable; at least it was intended to be subliminal and work as an extension to the architectural meanings, providing them with a penumbra of vague feeling.

Michael Graves has concentrated his attention on suggesting anthropomorphic metaphors without naming them. His elaboration of windows, doorways, and profiles, the erogenous zones of architecture, is conceived not just to call attention to their syntactical role, but also to dramatise the everyday human experience of familiar actions: standing beside a window ledge, holding it and gazing; noticing the visual juncture between the roof and the sky. The bodily metaphors are here much more general and implied. Indeed they may not even be perceived as such. But the constant attention to tight space, to touchable, close-grained details adds up to a consistent bodily experience and is an extensive field for metaphorical play. We naturally anthropomorphise the world in speech, and while this may be unacceptable science or the pathetic fallacy it is still fitting to give this ubiquitous activity a response in architecture. It of course does not yet constitute a full metaphysics and that realm remains a primary question mark for Post-Modernism. What indeed, beyond the human and animals realms, is architecture to be about?

213

214

Post-Modern Space

Modern architecture has often taken as its main subject matter the articulation of space, that is abstract space as *the* content of the form. The origins of this go to the nineteenth century and Germany when space, *Raum*, void etc. had a kind of metaphysical priority: not only was space the essence of architecture, its ultimate stuff, but also each culture expressed its will and existence through this medium. Sigfried Giedion's 'space-concepts' are the culmination of this tradition, just as are the Bauhaus, the Barcelona Pavilion and the Villa Savoye — which illustrated Giedion's ideas of transparency and 'space-time' perception. Another tradition of modern space, perhaps stronger, comes through the 'rational' Chicago frame and its development by Le Corbusier in the domino block. Here space is seen as isotropic, homogeneous in every direction, although layered in grids at right angles to the frontal plane and floor lines. The ultimate development of this 'warehouse' space is with the vast, enclosed halls of Mies and his followers. Besides being isotropic, it can be characterised as abstract limited by boundaries or edges, and rational or logically inferable from part to whole, or whole to part.

As opposed to this, Post-Modern space is historically specific, rooted in conventions, unlimited or ambiguous in zoning and 'irrational' or transformational in its relation of parts to whole. The boundaries are often left unclear, the space extended infinitely without apparent edge. Like the other aspects of Post-Modernism it is however evolutionary not revolutionary and thus it contains Modernist qualities — particularly the 'layering' and 'compaction composition' developed by Le Corbusier.[56] His La Roche house, 1923, develops several of the key Post-Modern themes: back-lighting, punched-out, screen space, and the implication of infinite extension created by overlapping planes. To these formal motifs Venturi added the skew or distorted space, created by sharp angles which exaggerate perspective. Both he and Eisenman increased the complexity of Le Corbusier's compaction composition. Where there were a few, bold elements juxtaposed there became a major traffic accident of collisions, where a few cardboard cutouts existed the walls became carved up like paper-dolls, and layered on top of each other like a patch-work quilt. If Le Corbusier's space is the equivalent of a Cubist collage, then Post-Modern space is as dense and rich as a Schwitters' *Merz*. Indeed one could say it developed partly if indirectly from Kurt Schwitters' great Merzbuild, the column of memories that he constructed inside his house, which was a literal accretion of every aspect of his life (unfortunately the assemblage was destroyed by the Nazis).

Yet in spite of this free-form precedent, and the Expressionist spaces of Hans Scharoun, Post-Modern space is more an elaboration of the Cartesian grid than an organic ordering. Thus Eisenman's or Graves' houses always keep a mental coordinate system no matter how free-form and baroque they become. The reference plane is always an implied frontality, and the route through the

215
216

215, 216 PETER EISENMAN, *House III for Robert Miller*, Lakeville, 1971. A careful collision at 45° of structure, volume, function, space, wardrobes, and what-have-you. Following through these collisions rigorously makes you look for and expect the presence, or absence, of a diagonal. This is an architecture of implication, where once you know what is implied you can follow the game. (Martin Tornallyay).

147

Opposite

217, 218 ROBERT STERN and JOHN HAGMANN, *Westchester Residence*, Armonk, NY, 1974–6. Pool front with fragmented signs relating to classical architecture, Frank Lloyd Wright, and Tuscany (the light ochre paint is stopped by a thin, virtual cornice of two red bands). An odd scale and tension are set up with the woods and rusticated base: the stuccoed wall seems too small and thin for the base and as if it would be blown away into the woods. This fragility and delicacy is set up in such great contrast that it may be termed mannerist, frustrating. See page 123.

Opposite above

219 REM KOOLHAAS and ZOE ZENGHELIS, *The City of the Captive Globe,* 1972. This version of what New York City is trying to do – capture the world's ideologies and styles – is a kind of eclecticism and pluralism by juxtaposition. The multiple coding is delightful, but the purity of each block is less so (although of course intended by the authors). Expressionism confronts Le Corbusier, Malevitch is at odds with Mies, and no dialogue ensues as the superblocks float around in their mutual isolation. Nonetheless the recognition of plural ideologies is a precondition for a Radical Eclecticism and public realm – even if it isn't realised here. The renewed interest in architectural drawing and painting culminated in 1977 with many exhibitions and books; Post-Modernists borrowed the graphic techniques of Archigram for anti-Futurist purposes. See page 128.

Opposite below left

220 CHARLES JENCKS, *Garagia Rotunda,* Wellfleet, 1977. Architecture as prefabrication plus cosmetics. The prefabricated garage, doors, ornament, pediments etc. were all chosen out of a catalogue, the same Cape Cod catalogue and the initial studio was constructed without supervision. Because the techniques and material were all traditional, the shell cost a minimal $5,500, and so the rest of the available money could be spent on cosmetics, on rectifying mistakes, on articulating the basic garage. Level changes, 'widow's walk', bay window, porch, entry gate, and interior harmonics were added to the basic shell. The view shows the entry head with its seven doors and twice-broken-split pediment, which articulates the actual door of entry. **See page 128.**

Opposite below right

221 *Garagia Rotunda,* entry gate which mediates several times the passage from inside to outside. The ocean and pond can be seen from the traditional 'widow's walk', and since the sky is also varying blue, six different shades of this colour were used on the outside, plus a strong red to mark the power box (top left). The gate reaches out visually into the green shrubs and cuts them up into rectangular slices framed in thick blue. With the passage of the sun the different hues switch their relative density, and the darker becomes brighter than the lighter ones. Classical elements are here ordered according to De Stijl principles of asymmetry.

building or the curvilinear elements then relate to this conceptual cage.

Eisenman's House 6 is, of course, supremely Modernist in its rigid exclusion of every contextual fact: there are no indications of the regional style, the strong colonial clapboard tradition, the woodland setting, the Frank family that inhabit it, or even their books, paintings and memorabilia (rather hard for a photographer and his wife, an art historian). The building could be upside-down or tilted on its side and it wouldn't make much difference (especially since columns hang in tension six inches from the ground and a stairway runs downside-up in mirror image). But the space and certain humorous touches are definitely Post-Modern: not only the Escher-like tricks I have mentioned, but also the play on the transformations of syntactic elements, particularly the column.

Columns are painted shades of grey and off-white – anything but a colour – to sometimes indicate their load-bearing role, or their mechanical function, or their decorative use, or for no reason. Walking through the house one becomes sensitised to these variations, and the game of architectural chess commences. The column may be in one of the four states mentioned above, or as its path is implied throughout the mental grid-system, it may be present or absent, or, and this is most extraordinary, it may be continued as a rectangular cut in the

222 PETER EISENMAN, *Two steps of transformation* drawing for House VI, one can see the stairs, real and virtual existing in counterpoint, the two reference planes, real and virtual, and the underlying presence or absence of the column grid. The general grid layering is kept throughout, thus continuing the movement in frontal and 90° turns, but there is a slight shift of reference planes on the diagonal, 45°.

223 *The absent column* marching through ceiling, roof and floor divides the marital bed. Originally the gap opened right up into the living room below.

121

224, 225 ROBERT STERN and JOHN HAGMANN, *Pool House*, Greenwich, Connecticut, 1973-4. Relating to the parent house in some details and the Shingle Style in others, this little folly celebrates the sun and water, through orientation and rippling rhythms. A double-height porch rotates to the view; the entrance to the left curves in under a colonnade (of three columns) which have odd, very odd, capitals. The column, beam and roof systems have undergone, like Eisenman's, several complicated transformations which are fun to mentally unravel. (Ed Stoecklein).

226 *Pool House* interior is very light and capricious because of the variety of skylights – a literal metaphor for following the sun's movement. The space pivots and undulates around the fireplace to the right, and is broken into by the column line and stairs at the left. A subtle tension is created between the reference wall, its grid and these distortions. (Ed Stoecklein).

surface. This *absent* column cuts through roof, wall and even floor, wreaking its ultimate havoc on domesticity (such is Eisenman's sardonic hatred of function). It divides the marital bed in two. A false step or leap and you'd land in the living room, or would have until the Franks glazed over the hole made by their absent column. Because of their unexpected baby (unexpected by the designer that is), who occupies the living room, several open areas have now been acoustically shielded by plexiglass; other spatially flowing tricks remain, however.

Again the column has its revenge, and again in the master bedroom, by transforming itself into a door. Ever seen a door as a column which rotates? And in three shades of grey and white? It's easy to calculate the snag. When the column is 'closed' there is still about two feet of left-over open space letting in all that kitchen smoke, guest gossip and baby talk. But if I've made this sound totally undesirable it's unintentional, because this pivoting column which is 'not a door/door' is startling and beautiful as a volumetric object and very amusing in its context. As a single conceit it may be questionable, but as the transformation of a theme well prepared for in advance, it's delightful and even sensual. One of the unlikely things about this building, at least it surprised me, is that the internal coding, the consistency of interrelated meanings created *ex nihilo*, made up for the lack of any external, historical coding, the conventional signs which architecture usually depends on for meaning. While the Purist language of Eisenman may be Modernist, his witty semantic use of this language is Post-Modern; while his exclusive concern for syntax and contempt for function are Modern, the ambiguity and sensuality of his spatial invention are Post-Modern.

Robert Stern, a *soi-disant* Post-Modernist, is by contrast actually quite Modern, or at least Moderne. All of his work has the linear, cardboard quality of the International Style behind it; all of it makes use of vast planes of pure, white wall separated by primary colours and good taste graphic abstractions. They may defer towards the vulgar and Art Deco, because Stern believes in the importance of Route 66 and 'inclusivism' (he was taught by Venturi at Yale), but he can't get over his inherent fastidiousness. Basically Stern has the sensibility of a New York cosmopolite crossed with an enlightened dilettante from Lord Burlington's circle, and his natural inclinations would drive him towards the Country House Set not Main Street; but his theory steers him sideways in more pluralist directions. (It seems at first surprising that Eisenman, a 'White' and Stern a 'Grey' should be smoothing over their non-colour ideologies to co-edit the writings of Philip Johnson, until one understands they are all, first, New Yorkers, and second, of related sensibility).

The Pool House Stern has built near its slightly colonial mother house, shows an appreciation for the local context and has historical allusions, two aspects he singles out to define Post-Modernism. It does not indulge in much applied ornament, his third definition, and actually concentrates on spatial and syntactic transformation à la Eisenman to become a very Modernist building indeed. And yet the Shingle Style, the complexities of roofscape and skylighting, the masterful use of the indirect, back-lit bow shape are not found in rational architecture. One cannot infer the detached column from the regular column grid, nor the distortions in entry and stairs – these are circumstantial articulations that, by varying from the norm, call attention to themselves. In other words it is

227 ROBERT STERN, *Westchester House*. Applied, painted decorative cornice set off against structural decorative trellis, that is traditional versus modern ornament. The slight, wavy curve is also contrasted with the close straight frame. (Ed Stoecklein).

228 *Westchester Residence,* interior looking at the fire place with indirect lighting from behind and punched out ambiguous space reminiscent of Lutyens.

heterogeneous not repeated space, modified to communicate a message of entry way or passage, gutter or calculated nonsense.

Stern's residence in Westchester County also continues the wit and absurdity of Post-Modernism, but combines these with a corpus of modern motifs: careful asymmetries slide across an off-white (light ochre) plane; there's an absence of sills and of decorative articulation except for the two bands of red at the top (a diminutive cornice, or misplaced stringcourse?). There's a Wrightian podium of flat-chested, fieldstone terraces, again without the copings and horizontal ornaments one would expect in a more traditional building. The interior, with its bold splashes of colour used to accentuate volume, could be an Art Deco version of a Le Corbusier, so pure, light and undecorated is it. Thus the Post-Modern architect by name is, as my litany insists, indelibly schizophrenic, tainted with a sensibility of Modernism which he will not throw off, yet picking up eclectic fragments where he wants.

The notion of 'fragments' is as important to Stern as it is to Graves, and it becomes a kind of compositional method in both of their hands. The south facade is partially unified by broken S-curves and by broken stringcourses and planes in shear, that is to say fragmented motifs lifted from the Baroque and Edwin Lutyens. The plan contains semi-circles, semi-ovals, semi-rectangles and a semi-spine of circulation, that is to say 'semi-forms' rather than completed ones, forms that, as in Zen aesthetics, demand a completion in the imagination.

217
218

218

229

229 *Westchester interior space* is stretched along a major axis that connects the master bedroom (7) to the sunporch (9). Parallel with this axis are five minor planes of space, also layered frontally to the entrance (1). The way space is brought in and out across these axes is delightful, if hard to read: curving wall disappears into a colonnade and screen to emerge again as a curving wall.

Legend
1 Entry
2 Living
3 Dining
4 Kitchen
5 Guest wing
6 Maids' rooms
7 Master bedroom
8 Conservatory
9 Sunporch
10 Bedroom

230 *Chinese garden space* is, like Post-Modern space, ambiguous, fragmented and eternally changing, but at the same time more precisely delineated through conventions. Here one of many walls is punctured by a 'moon gate' whose sign, the circle, also symbolises money and perfection. These meanings are further reinforced by the greyness of the wall so that, at dusk, the hole glows brightly as the 'moon who washes her soul' in the pool beyond. Other representational elements include the rockery and bushes (landscape painting) and writing above the door ('night time'). Precisely because the signs are traditional they have a wider base than the esoteric and fast-changing ones of Post-Modernism. (Maggie Keswick).

231 CHARLES MOORE and WILLIAM TURNBULL, *Faculty Club*, Santa Barbara, 1968. Punched-out walls, which are lit from behind, suggest a rich layering of space and a certain mystery as to its extent. The ambiguity of spatial cues juxtaposed with traditional signs — tapestry, neon banners — is typically Post-Modern.

The handling of space is equally suggestive and diffuse — none of the obvious unities of modern architecture, but everywhere complex implications which always lead on to a climax that is never present. There is an undeniable frustration to this, both mental and psychological, used as we are to a strong 'sense of an ending' and graspable whole. In part the parallel must be with the decentralised space of Mannerism, with its self-conscious ambiguity and contradictory spatial cues. In fact C. Ray Smith has termed recent American architecture 'Supermannerist' because of the plethora of spatial tricks — the omnipresent diagonals, violent scale changes, supergraphics and whimsical punctuation.[58] The comparison of Post-Modern with Mannerist space is helpful in many ways, but I think there is another analogous model, one of a quasi-religious nature.

Post-Modern, like Chinese garden space, suspends the clear, final ordering of events for a labyrinthine, rambling 'way' that never reaches an absolute goal. The Chinese garden crystallises a 'liminal' or in-between space that mediates between pairs of antinomies, the Land of the Immortals and the world of society being the most obvious mediation.[59] It suspends normal categories of time and space, social and rational categories which are built up in everyday architecture and behaviour, to

become 'irrational' or quite literally impossible to figure out. In the same manner Post-Modernists complicate and fragment their planes with screens, non-recurrent motifs, ambiguities and jokes to suspend our normal sense of duration and extent. The difference, and it is a profound one, is that the Chinese garden had an actual religious and philosophical metaphysics behind it, and a built up conventional system of metaphor, whereas our complicated architecture has no such accepted basis of signification. Our metaphysics often remains private, as in the Surrational creations of John Hejduk. Thus, although Post-Modern space may be in every way as rich and ambiguous as Chinese garden space, it cannot articulate the depth of meaning with the same precision. Its metaphorical and metaphysical bases are just being laid, and it is questionable how far they can grow in an industrial society.

Charles Moore is, in his own way, trying to develop an architecture of public metaphor and his work, which pulls together practically all the themes of Post-Modernism, shows the possibilities and present limits of this approach. Moore has written about Hadrian's villa and the importance of images and historical allusion in creating a sense of place, so he is well qualified to design for the public realm.[60] His Kresge College dormitories combine many historical memories that are only vaguely presented — alluded to rather than precisely quoted. The overall plan meanders and shifts violently, a cross between the serpentine walk through a Chinese garden and a tight Italian hill town.

230

231

232

232 CHARLES MOORE and WILLIAM TURNBULL, *Kresge College,* University of California at Santa Cruz, plan 1972–4. A meandering route threaded through a redwood forest has each plaza with a separate monument to define the 'place'. Many buildings set up their own axial and rhythmic systems rather like Hadrian's Villa (200), but here on a linear L-route. The sense of place was further underlined by creating opposite activities at two ends of the scheme – Post Office and entrance arena at bottom and assembly and dining areas at the top. Hence the street is well used and keeps students going from one side to the other. A complex water works and orange trees reinforce the Spanish image; 'a laundromat stands for the village well' unfortunately not having quite the same importance, and telephone kiosks are turned into major archways. (Morley Baer).

The image of the Mediterranean village is inescapable and reinforced by several cues: large white planes, a public, two storey arcade, angular junctions between volumes. But whereas the southern European village gives stability and a sense of permanence, because it is built of an encompassing stone, Kresge is made from a cardboard-like wood, that 'cheapskate' material that has always plagued Modernism. Thus a feeling of insubstantiality is created at the very point that the metaphor of enclosure is about to be consummated, and the image of the Italian hill town criticises, not reinforces, the meanings intended.

In like manner, the references to the Spanish Steps, the *Arc de Triomphe,* the cascades and waterways of the Alhambra – all memories Moore has collected on his many travels – call into question their present use. Is this a kind of *haute vulgarisation,* or the pastiche and travesty we have noted before? Perhaps the first. Moore has spoken, not pejoratively, about whimsy and nostalgia in architecture and this work has some of the virtues and vices of both these genres. On the negative side, we can see how the insubstantial feel of the place combines with its bright supergraphics and flimsy construction to lead to the student epithet, 'Clown Town'. There is always the danger with Moore's work that its relative cheapness will combine with the whimsy to produce a kind of tawdry pathos, like a run-down summer resort, but by and large these meanings are overtaken by the more powerful metaphors of place, which he has intended.

Thus Kresge mixes the very personal scale of a village with the calculated surprise of a walk through a garden – whether English or Chinese. The two storey arcade screens have varying syncopated rhythms, combined with syncopated colours behind them, to increase the feelings of suspense and discovery. Since, in plan, the buildings pinch in perspective they can heighten the sense of movement and depth; since various 'anti-monuments' punctuate the route – post office, laundromat, telephone altar etc. – there is some content, however banal, to anticipate. Moore has justified this low-keyed approach as fitting for the modest, egalitarian role of the student dormitory.

> . . . All the inhabitants are students, there for four or five years together. So it seemed important to us to establish not a set of institutional monuments along the street to help give a sense of place to the whole, and a sense of where one was in one's passage up the street, but rather to make a set of trivial monuments, of things like drainage ditches made into fountains, of the laundromat facade a speaker's rostrum with garbage collection under . . .[61]

This *bricolage,* an ironic debunking of the public realm, has the double meaning intended – to punctuate and define experience and to deflate pomposity – but one

233 *Kresge College* two storey arcade and entrance stairs, traditional elements which are slightly exaggerated here in scale as are the conventional number plaques. Complicated rhythms are set up which run through the whole scheme like a Mannerist *palazzo*: here ABCBCDBAC. The porches which serve for sunning and street watching, are painted underneath in strong primary reds and yellows. (Morley Baer).

125

longs, by contrast, for a modicum of public decorum, the straight gesture of communal well-being. Moore has studied the scenic planning of Disneyland and its stage-set quality has been successfully incorporated here, but at the cost of overwhelming normality.

Still, if we contrast this dormitory village with others built in the last forty years its virtues become very much apparent, even sacrosanct. As opposed to the Modern
18– university – Mies' IIT for instance – it is carefully set in its
22 context rather than dropped unceremoniously, like an urban bomb. Thus the backs of the buildings, in wood painted ochre, are sympathetic to the forest, and the plan slides this way and that to avoid existing redwoods. Op-posed to the predictable spaces of rational architecture,
234 there is always a twist and surprise around every corner and nook.

The depth of the metaphor involved here becomes greater on examination : 'place' results not just from strong images, but also from the careful distribution of activities. Since the post office and assembly areas are located at opposite ends of the L-shape there is a natural to and fro of movement that keeps the streets occupied, and since functions are fragmented and interspersed there are the chance encounters, and the richness, of the historic village. Thus the metaphors of place and community are created through use as well as image.

Moore has extended his type of public (sometimes whimsical) imagery in a more representational direction,
235 incorporating in one scheme for New Orleans precise iconography such as the boot of Italy, and a play on the real, historic orders (turning some metopes into fountains called 'wetopes'), but his most convincing Post-Modern building, to my mind, is the Burns house, for a professor at UCLA. Here the cut-out stage-sets, something of a Moore brandmark, have a perplexing mystery which is delightfully confusing but not frustrating. The walk through the house is peppered with surprises and other forms of architectural spice.

Each image that appears en route – a Mexican balcony,
182 an altar-like organ, inglenook etc – is at first the focus of visual attention and then, because of back lighting, merely the pretext for further discovery. The layering of cut-out walls has the same effect as that in Eisenman's work, providing the suggestion of infinity, except here many are set at a skew-angle, so that scale and orientation are dislocated. As you move up the stairway towards
236 the attic-study, two extraordinary mysteries unfold: the view back reveals a perspective distortion of such com-plexity that the relative scale and position of object are impossible to determine, while the route forward splits and then widens in reverse perspective (by 1971 a con-ventional motif).

This is the left-over, idiosyncratic stairway we might expect near the sanctum, the professor's lair, but then the lower route suddenly turns into an Art Deco dressing room. From Mexico through a church with its organ to an attic stair that reveals a Hollywood, back-stage dressing table – the images and moods are quite unexpected, but not in-appropriate. One looks in the first mirror, a natural stop on the walk, to admire one's finery, then the next – which turns out not to be a mirror at all, but a hole, cut and placed like the previous mirror. It opens over a drop of fifteen feet. This joke and use of human vanity is just another characteristic surprise of this Post-Modern space. Everywhere there are details of colour and form that remain to be discovered – eyetraps which can spring

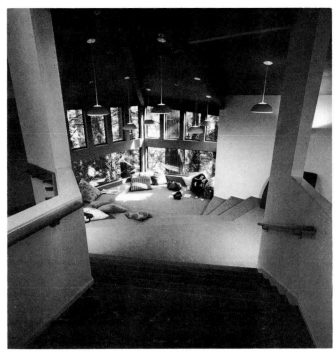

234 *Kresge College*, space spills from the library in a cascade of steps which focus on the corner and redwoods beyond – a typical 'skew' space of Post-Modernism. (Morley Baer).

235 CHARLES MOORE and WILLIAM HERSEY, *Piazza D'Italia*, New Orleans, 1976. An exedra made up from the different orders turns into a fountain in the shape of Italy (at the base). This scheme for the Italian community mixes supergraphics with classicism, bubbling water with architecture.

shut.

The outside, with its seventeen shades of reds and 181 oranges and earthcolours, is equally amusing and pro-found. Several shades are contrasted to give the effect of shadows where they don't exist, thus turning the corner on a volume where it doesn't. Other shades mark out a progression from dark to light, from the dull, underplayed tower to the more important, bright functions. But all these tonalities are so subtly related that they actually integrate and create a whole feeling of pleasant domes-ticity, appropriate for Southern California. Without specifically invoking the Spanish Mission Style and the other local associations, Moore has managed to design something equivalent in feeling yet superior in wit.

236 *Burns House*, section and plan. Space flows and zigzags to the private study at the top. Several walls are punched out and skewed off the right angle.

Conclusion – Radical Eclecticism?

If Post-Modern space continues to develop in this direction towards the mysterious, ambiguous and sensual, it will start to conventionalise certain metaphors of a quasi religious nature. There's not much chance these will ever be supported by a socially shared metaphysics, and so they will signify a general spirituality when not an obvious idiosyncrasy. What I would guess, but it's no better than other prophecies, is that the present developments towards complication and eclecticism would continue and that we might see an architecture emerge that is quite similar to the Neo-Queen Anne and Edwardian of eighty years ago. Every indication points towards increasing complication in formal and theoretical concerns: the work of Graves, Eisenman, Moore *et al.* is an elaboration of a 1920s syntax to the point of mannerism; on a completely different level the theories of Jane Jacobs and Herbert Gans point towards a corresponding heterogeneity of urban villagers and taste cultures. No doubt a case can be made for simplification and large-scale decisions concerning utilitarian structures such as roadways, but by and large the natural development of a city towards increasing complexity – a patchwork quilt of contradictions and mixed intentions – is positive, because it reflects the mixed desires and goals that any large metropolis must fulfil.

If one looks for a historical parallel, when many styles and ideologies were competing, the period 1870–1910 becomes even more pertinent, because then at least fifteen styles were in opposition (no doubt too many) and complication and eclecticism were rife. The general trend of all styles towards heterogeneity was reaching a peak – High Gothic couldn't get any more articulated or the Second Empire Style any more bombastic. If complexity was a natural metaphor for power, then there was no place more complicated to go than the Paris Opera – except to a thorough-going eclecticism, like the 'Queen Anne Style' as seen in Texas, Los Angeles and San Francisco. In fact all styles were hybrid and becoming syncretic if not eclectic – one only has to think of the borrowings between Art Nouveau and the Second Empire Style. Today precisely such borrowings are occurring, perhaps because all designers now belong to the world small-town of architectural magazines, and an idea in any backyard on the map soon spreads elsewhere – thanks to cheap, half-tone reproduction. Hence the fragmentation in design, not only the conscious 'fragments' of a Graves or Stern or Kroll, but also the natural one that comes from a compound set of sources. Furthermore, the return to the past has become something of a backwards race that might reach renaissance proportions: we only have to recapitulate the historicism of Venturi, the straight revivalisms of Disneyworlds, the Neo-Vernacular, Neo-Ornament and Contextualism – all point in the same direction, over the shoulder.

Finally, if our pattern books today include four hundred building systems, if 'local' materials now mean everything down at the hardware shop, then our natural vernacular is eclectic if not polyglot, and even the present attempt at a simple Neo-Vernacular is bound to be infected by these mixed sources. In semiotic terms, the *langue* (total set of communicational sources) is so heterogeneous and diverse that any singular *parole* (individual selection) will reflect this, even if only in excluding the diversity. Such are the facts of architectural production.

A corresponding argument can be made concerning consumption. Any middle-class urbanite in any large city from Teheran to Tokyo is bound to have a well-stocked, indeed over-stocked, 'image-bank' that is continually restuffed by travel and magazines. His *musée imaginaire* may mirror the pot-pourri of the producers, but it is nonetheless natural to his way of life. Barring some kind of totalitarian reduction in the heterogeneity of production and consumption, it seems to me desirable that architects learn to use this inevitable heterogeneity of languages. Besides, it is quite enjoyable. Why, if one can afford to live in different ages and cultures, restrict oneself to the present, the locale? Eclecticism is the natural evolution of a culture with choice.

There are, however, objections. It is constantly pointed out that eclectic systems, both in philosophy and architecture, didn't produce much of originality, nor confront key issues with any kind of tenacity. The charge is that eclecticism is a kind of weak compromise, a mish-mash where second-rate thinkers can take refuge in a welter of confusing antinomies. They combine contradictory material in the hope of avoiding a difficult choice, or seeing through a problem to a creative conclusion.

Thus eclectics have been trimmers or dilettanti, and the architecture often botched. Furthermore, eclecticism in the nineteenth century was often motivated more by opportunism than conviction, and architects mixed their modes as much out of laxness as desire. We are all familiar with the vague pastiche, 'in the manner of'

127

237 J. CATHER NEWSOM, *1330 Carroll Street*, Los Angeles, c. 1888. A twelve room house with 'Californian' ornament, lacy spindle and lattice in the 'Moorish manner'. The elaborate shingle patterns, stained glass, circular contrasts and eave recessions add a depth and grandeur to entry. Such virtuosity in wood was helped by the great carpenter-builder tradition which already existed. The results, like Charles Moore's, were not as expensive as they look, and equally wide in reference.

238 HOUSE on 309 STEINER STREET, San Francisco, c. 1890. The 'Queen-Anne Style' was the last great attempt to merge different styles and incorporate disparate material. Various elements are collaged together with great skill: a bay window is transformed into a tower and two pediments, large curves are set against spindles and straight lines, decorative plasterwork against wood. Thousands of these carpenter-built houses survive in San Francisco, a testimony that inexpensive building needn't be dull nor without ornament.

Something, without being much of Anything. The motivation was essentially one of mood and comfort and while these are perfectly honourable goals, they certainly are not sufficient for architecture as a whole. There was little semantic and social argument involved, and hence nineteenth-century eclecticism was weak. Indeed, there was hardly any theory of eclecticism beyond choosing the right style for the job.

In contrast to this weak eclecticism, it seems to me that Post-Modernism has at least the potential to develop a stronger more radical variety. The various formal, theoretical and social threads are there, waiting to be drawn and woven together. Indeed, the seven aspects of Post-Modernism I have outlined do constitute such an amalgam, even if it isn't yet an interrelated whole. As I have constantly reiterated, there is room in this amalgam for Modernism, precisely because the theory of semiotics postulates meaning through opposition, and the possibility of rich meaning using a restricted language.[62]

By way of summary the common ground of the seven approaches can be stressed and an emergent Radical

140
239
219

Eclecticism can be projected as a possibility, an alternative to the weak eclecticism of the past.

A Radical Eclecticism would include areas of extreme simplicity and reduction, not only for their contrast in space, but also because of a dialectic in meaning over time. As opposed to the theory of Modernism, however, this reduction would never be more than momentary, or situational, depending on the particular context. It would be motivated by the original Greek meaning of eclectic – 'I select' – and follow the basically sensible course of selecting from all possible sources those elements which were most useful or pertinent *ad hoc*.

In a studio building on Cape Cod for instance, I selected elements from the existing vernacular, from traditional shingle construction and a basic catalogue of prefabricated building parts. The selection was a mixture of new and old, traditional balusters and modern pivot windows – all of which was local to the area and easy to build. The basic shell was a prefabricated garage (although finally hand-built) and the garage door was the cheapest way to get a large, framed opening (and the effect of a *baldacchino*).

220

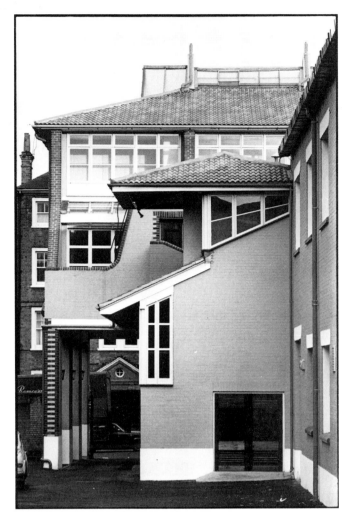

239 CAMPBELL, ZOGOLOVITCH, WILKINSON and GOUGH, *Phillips West 2, Residences and Offices*, London 1976. Art Deco mixed with London vernacular and pantiles create a melange which is suitable to this mixture of functions.

240 *Garagia Rotunda* interior with part of the harmonies visible. The 4 x 4 inch studs are painted differing shades of blue on their sides to bring out the 3/9/5 rhythm. The underlying symmetry and axes are brought out by blue tile lines, while corner angles are painted in *trompe l'oeil* to imitate a mirror image.

241 *Garagia Rotunda* plan, overlapping space modules, organised in a general S-line approach which ends in two cross-axes noted on the floor in blue tile. The space cells are more or less on a four foot module and layered in axes which intersect at right angles.

Since all the basic choices were absolutely minimal, inexpensive and based on builder's vernacular, the majority of the money could be spent on articulation, on changing levels, and painting harmonic colour combinations. I wouldn't claim this studio as a model of Radical Eclecticism — the program was too limited for one thing — but it does have the mixture of languages and can be read by the local inhabitants (for instance those who built it while I wasn't there).

There are, I think, no completely convincing examples of Radical Eclecticism in existence, besides the venerable buildings of Antonio Gaudí; just hints of what it might be adumbrated by designers such as Bruno Reichlin in Switzerland, or Thomas Gordon Smith in California. In general, however, some of its aspects have now clarified.

Unlike Modernism it makes use of the full spectrum of communicational means — metaphorical and symbolic as well as spatial and formal. Like traditional eclecticism it selects the right style, or subsystem, where it is appropriate — but a Radical Eclecticism mixes these elements within one building. Thus the semantic overtones to each style are mapped to their closest functional equivalents — for instance in Thomas G. Smith's work the entrance and porch are given classical formality whereas the sides are in the vernacular of the region.

The examples cited are just individual houses and therefore too restricted in their coding and breadth of expression. At the present time a larger model is needed, greater in scope and urban — for instance an apartment house in the inner city, which could take into account the existing local codes.

Theoretically at least several of the key issues are clear. One must start by defining a basic opposition in coding between the inhabitant and professional, perhaps taking as one departure point Basil Bernstein's fundamental distinction between 'restricted' and 'elaborated' codes.[63] As mentioned above (pages 55–62) the varying codes based on semiotic groups may not be determined by class alone, but are usually a complex mixture of ethnic

242 BRUNO REICHLIN and FABIO REINHARDT, *Maison Tonini*, Torricella Switzerland, 1972–4. A well-proportioned villa in the Alberti/Palladian tradition, with grand arch framing view, symmetrical axes, and very simple mathematical harmonies (visible here is ABA'CA'BA and C = A + B). The finish and furnishings are unnecessarily prison-like, but one assumes this is a momentary Calvinism and will not last with these young designers.

243 *Maison Tonini, split axonometric.* The authors quote Alberti — '. . . the ''heart of the house'' is the basic part, around it are grouped the subordinate parts as if it were a public square within the building.' Thus the repetitive square rooms must be seen as little houses clustered around the central heart, the piazza, where the family eat around their round table. (Heinrich Helfenstein).

background, age, history and locale. The designer should logically start with an investigation of the semiotic group and always keep in his mind the varying views of the good life as seen by the people involved since architecture ultimately signifies a way of life — something not entirely understood by the Modern Movement. The training necessary for this needn't entail a degree in anthropology. Common sense, a willingness to understand the client's background plus a certain appreciation of etiquette can suffice. Social research may help. Sympathy and constant consultation are minimum requirements. The difficulty is that since continuous traditions have been broken, and the profession has its own language and ideology, one cannot assume a commonalty of values and architectural language, so an inevitable self-conscious theory must suffice to link this duality.

In any case, the designer should first study the area, the language of the tribe, and understand it fully before designing. The language may have an ethnic or cultural dimension based on the background of the inhabitants and also a purely architectural dimension — the vernacular (which has usually been disrupted, but elements of which usually exist). The kinds of thing that can be said in this traditional language will conserve the values of the local group. Indeed such a conservative approach is the *sine qua non* for any urban development, for the reasons that preservations, the 'contextualists' and Conrad Jameson advance (see above pages 107–109). But this traditional base does not exhaust the questions as they sometimes argue.

In several studies concerning the way architecture is perceived I've found an underlying schizophrenia in interpretations which, I believe, parallels the essentially dual nature of the architectural language. [64] Generally speaking there are two codes, a popular, traditional one which like spoken language is slow-changing, full of clichés and rooted in family life, and secondly a modern one full of neologisms and responding to quick changes in technology, art and fashion as well as the avant-garde of architecture. One code is likely to be preferred by any individual, but quite likely both, contradictory codes exist in the same person. Since an architect is, by profession and daily work, necessarily responsive to fast-changing codes — and these of course include literal building codes — one can see why he has been alienated from the slow-changing languages, and Modernism has had such an ideological hold on his mind. It simplified his problem considerably to a professional one of communication between specialists. Architectural conferences and magazines necessarily celebrate specialist values, and architecture as an art addresses itself to an even smaller elite, the 'happy few' who are concerned to make subtle distinctions and perpetuate the art — not a minor achievement. Since there is an unbridgeable gap between the elite and popular codes, the professional and traditional values, the modern and vernacular language, and since there is no way to abolish this gap without a drastic curtailment in possibilities, a totalitarian manoeuvre, it seems desirable that architects recognise the schizophrenia and code their buildings on two levels. Partly this will parallel the 'high'

244, 245 *Maison Tonini*, hall first floor looking out onto distant view framed between an arch and 'small houses' (pediments) to either side. The left one is a kind of inglenook, for reading next to a fireplace. The Mackintosh chairs and their place in the centre around the round dining table constitute the larger public house within the house; it goes up three storeys and is lit at the top. (Heinrich Helfenstein).

and 'low' versions of classical architecture, but it will not be, as that was, an homogeneous language. Rather the double coding will be eclectic and subject to the heterogeneity that makes up any large city. Partly this is the 'inclusivism' that Venturi, Stern and Moore call for, but in addition it asks for more precise local or traditional coding than they have yet undertaken. Their work still gives priority to esoteric, fast-changing codes and treats traditional ones, often, as an opportunity for historical allusion.

Radical Eclecticism by contrast starts design from the tastes and languages prevailing in any one place and overcodes architecture (with many redundant cues) so that

246 PHILIP C. JOHNSON, *AT & T Building*, New York City, 1978–82, called the first 'major monument of post-modernism' by Paul Goldberger, it may well represent the grave of the movement to detractors. Basically a glass and steel skyscraper is shrunk to a grandfather's clock and imprisoned within a granite cage – Serlio at the bottom, Chippendale 'refeenment' at the top. Such dual coding – half modern, half trad – may be annoying to both taste cultures, although the codes are being marginally extended (e.g. the granite sheathing acts as an environmental cover, and the Ledouxian hole at the top will emit exhaust). One has to recall Johnson's 'follee' called 'the most sincerely hated building' by the British because it had an androgynous slickness. Beyond the controversy however is an interesting possibility: the skyscraper might loose its bland, economic coding and return to its former position as a major fantasy form of capital (whether capitalist or socialist).

247 THOMAS GORDON SMITH, *Jefferson Street House* project, Berkeley, California, 1976. Like Queen Anne and Maybeck's work, an easy-going mixture of grand, traditional elements with the local vernacular. The 'Palladian' viewing porch treated as a symmetrical, formal front which organises the informal, rambling sides; meaning through opposition.

248 THOMAS GORDON SMITH, *Paulownia House,* Oakland, California, 1977. A prefabricated Quonset hut, wood frame construction and a rusticated, Serlio arch which is mirrored to make it whole. The quoins, voussoirs and other traditional elements are made from stock pieces to suggest a more substantial construction than actually exists.

it can be understood and enjoyed by different taste cultures – both the inhabitants and the elite. Although it starts from these codes, it doesn't necessarily use them to send the expected messages, or ones which simply confirm the existing values. In this sense it is both contextual and dialectical, attempting to set up a discourse between different and often opposed taste cultures.

Although it is generated in participation with those who will use the building, it transcends their goals and may even criticise them. For these contrasting reasons it can be read on at least two quite distinct levels telling parallel stories which may or may not be consistent,

depending on the context and building involved.

Finally Radical Eclecticism is multivalent, as against so much Modern architecture: it pulls together different kinds of meaning, which appeal to opposite faculties of the mind and body, so that they interrelate and modify each other. The taste of the building, its smell and touch, engage the sensibility as much as does the sight and contemplation. In a perfectly successful work of architecture – that of Gaudí – the meanings add up and work together in the deepest combination. We aren't there yet, but a tradition is growing which dares make this demand for the future.

Postscript – Towards Radical Eclecticism

Since I finished the revised edition of this book in 1978 several important shifts in architecture have occurred which have led to this postscript. Major Modern architects such as Hans Hollein and James Stirling have now gone convincingly 'Post' in every way but name; major American practitioners in New York and Chicago have changed direction in a dramatic turnabout leaving their previous faith in favour of the new creed; finally, important schemes have been built and, in one case, the Piazza d'Italia, the real 'major monument' to Post-Modernism is nearing completion. This book has had the (editorial) misfortune to be written just as Post-Modernism was becoming a world movement with developments occurring faster than new editions.

The situation is dynamic with sudden bursts of the new architecture arising in unexpected places such as Japan and Chicago, places where Modern and Late-Modern architecture have a strong following. Indeed some architects like Helmut Jahn and Philip Johnson vary from one building to the next, from Late to Post and back to Modern – a confusing course to follow at least for the public, and one which has led me elsewhere to classify the three schools according to thirty variables.[65] There is no reason here to elaborate such a complex taxonomy. Just the basic distinction should be kept in mind: Late-Modern architecture is an exaggeration of several Modern concerns such as the technological image of a building, its circulation, logic and structure, whereas Post-Modern architecture, in an attempt to communicate, is double-coded, an eclectic mix of traditional or local codes with Modern ones.

The shift to Post-Modernism has occurred most strongly in the United States, a natural situation given the presence of the major protagonists as well as a relatively favourable building climate where experiments are welcomed. Now underway are at least three multi-million dollar commissions, those leviathans which gave Modernism such a bad name: Philip Johnson's AT & T building previously mentioned, Hardy, Holzman and Pfeiffer's Willard Hotel addition in Washington DC and Ulrich Franzen's Philip Morris Corporate Headquarters in New York. In each case the size and generality of the building task have led to muted results only marginally more articulated than their predecessors. The mixture of Modern and Revivalist styles is smoothed over; sharp contrasts are avoided; imagery, ornament and historical allusion are present but subdued. The same can be said of the recent Chicago Post-Modernism of the large corporate practices: Peter Pran's skyscraper designed within the firm of Schmidt, Garden and Erickson and Helmut Jahn's work within C. F. Murphy Associates. The intermixture of codes is subtle and understated, a predictable fusion for large offices and conservative clients. More surprising is that this mixture has a refreshingly naive aspect. Crisply detailed and extremely archetypal in its use of historical form (*the* semi-circle, *the* cornice, etc) it seems at the start of a new tradition, not unlike Brunelleschi's first use of classical details. Forms are not used expressively (beyond their representational role), they are not articulated or shaped with sculptural weight. Instead they are treated as flat appliqué, or melded into the flat surface of a building becoming thereby equated with constructional necessity.

With the work of the Chicago Seven,[66] more particularly Thomas Beeby, we find an almost inevitable conjunction

249 ULRICH FRANZEN, *Philip Morris Corporate Headquarters*, New York City, 1979–82. Classical skyscraper design on Grand Central Station side, with base (echoing Station), vertical shaft and capital. The mouldings, echelon and cut-out loggia repeat the centralising symmetry of the base. To the side street the building presents a modern, horizontal facade; the meeting of this literal double-coding might have produced a more ironic corner joint. (Ulrich Franzen Associates).

250 HELMUT JAHN with C. F. MURPHY ASSOCIATES, *Agricultural Engineering Sciences Building*, Urbana, 1979– . Brick and decorative trim relating to the existing campus buildings, are treated as a flat, symbolic surface laid over a glass background building. The flat, notional and literal handling of detail, stretched over a proportional grid, is reminiscent of Brunelleschi. (C. F. Murphy Associates).

of Neo-Palladianism and Neo-Mies, elegant in its crisp detailing and refined structuring of space. Beeby's Townhouse, produced as one in a row of varying contextual buildings, mixes Modern structural grid with traditional aedicules and barrel vaults. The classicism inherent in Mies is so close to Neo-Palladianism that when they are forced to meet in Beeby's work the conjunction seems natural; an inevitable consequence of Palladian rules being followed in reinforced concrete and steel. Beeby also mixes iconography in a thoroughgoing manner so that the grotesque face of Hades in the basement grotto seems at home with the polished chrome dragster on the ground floor. The strength of this work is its sure handling of structure and complex spatial rhythms which read horizontally and vertically in syncopation. Each 'internal facade' becomes a variation on the previous one and on the front *Serliana*. The ornament, such as it is, results directly from constructional elements particularly the mullion, and in this way provides another bridge between Modern and traditional practice. It's as if Mies had gone Post-Modern, or at least back to his Schinkel period.

Perhaps the most important aspect of these townhouses is that they return to the American street tradition by combining individual variation within an overall street morphology. This tradition (which exists notably in San Francisco, Chicago and New York) was one broken by Modernism. The Chicago townhouses, variants of which are being built now, show an elegant handling of stripped classical detail and ornament that re-establishes an urban grain and incident. In Europe similar types of scheme have evolved with less individual expression of each house, and in London one version of this infill architecture has been completed. Jeremy Dixon has designed a scheme which fits into the nineteenth-century urban pattern both in plan and detail. Accepting the street lines and traditional layout, the bay windows of adjoining houses and their emphasis on the front door, the scheme manages to be both acceptably familiar and inventive. The inhabitants can recognise their traditional language and requirements; the stereotypes are used in a relatively straightforward way, as stock as the London brick with which it is built.

But then, on further inspection, there are esoteric meanings more directly accessible to the architect, or the inhabitant who cares to search for them: the physiognomic visage, the suggestion of a face, which is appropriately made by the front door (or rather two front doors combined over the traditional stoop). This 'face' is also another favourite image of Post-Modernists, an aedicule, a 'little house', the signifier of domesticity which has had such a long history in the West since its first conventional-isation in ancient Greece. The aedicule as a form is masterfully repeated at different scales – in the windows, roof profiles and 'entrance gates' – to unite a complex array of formal quotes. These vary from the Neo-Vernacular brick to the Dutch gable with its crow-step articulation, from Art Deco ziggurats to Rationalist grids. Particularly ingenious is the way the aedicular gate-post becomes a cover for garbage cans on the house side.

In one respect this scheme epitomises a search of Post-Modernists for a rich, flexible language which stems from the locale. It is an eclectic language as mixed as the Queen Anne of a century ago and as responsive to particular cultural conditions. The attempt to derive such a language has been made by other architects in Amsterdam

251 THOMAS BEEBY, *Townhouse Project*, Chicago, 1978. Based on Palladio's Villa Poiana, like Isozaki's Post-Modern work, with archetypal circles, rectangles and flat decorative detail, this townhouse also incorporates a Miesian structural logic on a five foot module. A sequence of varying spatial character is defined with barrel vault, a dome over the stair and subterranean grotto. (Thomas Beeby).

252 'CHICAGO SEVEN', *Townhouse Projects*, Chicago, 1978. Like a traditional nineteenth-century American street these houses keep the urban morphology but vary the detail, ornament and colour. Note again the archetypal use of circles, pediments, rectangles and flat structuring modules. (Stanley Tigerman).

253 JEREMY DIXON, *St. Marks Road*, London, 1976–9. Twenty-four houses and twenty flats placed on a tight site pick up the existing Edwardian street pattern and scale. By doubling the houses in a single, visual unit the appearance of a large house is kept; the angled plan, while an economic use of the site, produces odd internal conditions.

and Vienna, notably by the group called Missing Link. These young designers have undertaken empirical studies of pre-existing urban signs — the towers, gates, doors, street corners and courtyards of Vienna. Elegant line-drawings are made of these recurrent motifs — 'words' of the Viennese architectural language — and a new set of typologies is derived from them through a process of abstraction. Perhaps their design results do not yet completely make the hoped for 'missing link' with the past, but their analyses show one way of proceeding towards that goal.

The contextualists (above, page 110) are also headed towards a regional historicism without, however, approaching too close to traditional syntax. Leon Krier's designs for Rome, and the other schemes produced for the show 'Roma Interrotta', summer 1978, are both contextual and disruptive, based on the Nolli plan of Rome and opposed to its grain. Krier has, in typical Rationalist manner, reinvented the 'primitive hut' of columns and triangular roof truss, but this time each column is the side of an eight-storey tower and the pyramidal roof encloses an awesome public realm — a cross between a train-shed and an open-air market. The

255 MISSING LINK, (Otto Kapfinger and Adolf Krischanitz), *Vienna Studies*, 1977. A series of elegant line drawings of typical Viennese buildings, here the *Wohnhöfe* (the public housing of the twenties), abstracts recurrent aspects of the local language — the towers, gates, corners, courtyards etc. From these studies a new eclectic whole is created which relates to the past. (Missing Link).

254 JEREMY DIXON, *St. Marks Road*, London, 1976–9. Slight variations in stained glass and door colour give perceptible individuality to each house. The aedicular 'face' is repeated at different scales, in windows, gateway and roof pitch, providing variations on this domestic theme. The variety of texture and small scale elements also reinforce this theme.

256 LEON KRIER, *Rione project*, Rome, 1978, for the Via Condotti and Via Corso. An international centre and airport terminal are among the functions projected for this monument to a new public realm. Krier, as other Rationalists, both uses and distorts the existing language and morphology of the city producing heroic images of a yet unborn society. The mixture of primitive construction and sophisticated technology is as striking as the contrasts with Piranesi. (Leon Krier).

257 GEORGIA BENAMO and CHRISTIAN DE PORTZAMPARC, *Rue des Hautes-Formes*, Paris, 1975–9. Hanging arches, a 'thick wall' with various window types and a plan which acknowledges the street and central public realm; otherwise the scheme resembles modernist slab blocks in many ways.

258 JAMES STIRLING, *Staatsgalerie and Chamber Theatre*, Stuttgart, 1977, construction 1979–1980. One moves under an entrance arch, a primitive hut, but then to left or right off axis. The U-shaped, symmetrical gallery is in front, but one has to approach it diagonally up a ramp; the circular, open-air sculpture court can be reached on axis, but one moves through it on a perimeter, semi-circular ramp. This connects up finally with a walkway into the more domestic urban fabric. In this circuitous way the public is brought informally right into the heart of the museum without actually gaining entry. Should they wish to see the paintings another entrance is provided leading to a straightforward, chronological journey through the history of art. Thus basic antinomies, circle and square, frontality and rotation, informality and formal viewing are acknowledged. (John Donat).

Opposite

259, 260 MICHAEL GRAVES, *Sunar Showroom*, Merchandise Mart, Chicago, 1979. The display of furniture in an inside space cut off from natural light and familiar views. To provide some location to this abstract space Graves has layered it with a series of screens, and provided a certain expectancy and surprise. The figure of Terminus in low relief culminates one axis, while exaggerated 'upside-down' columns and lighting troughs provide further identity.

261 ELIA ZENGHELIS and OMA, *Hotel Sphinx*, New York City, 1975. Anthropomorphic imagery animates a potentially overpowering scale. Like the Hyatt Hotels springing up across America, but with considerably more wit and colour, this scheme mixes various urban functions. The legs are escalators, the tails are twin towers, the head that 'turns and stares' at important civic events is a health club – the whole animal is a 'luxury hotel designed as a model for mass housing'. A very rational approach to existing urban fantasy – surrationalism in fact.

drawings, when seen collaged into the Roman perspectives of Piranesi, actually stand up to these grand and disturbing images. The public buildings have the breadth of scale and heavy gestural quality typical of the Roman tradition. They are meant to support a local form of civic organisation, the *rione*, an alternative to the centralised bureaucracy and state. Each one would have restaurants, clubs, rooms for games and large top-floor studios for artists who would fabricate the syndicalist imagery.[67] The idea, as Krier describes it, is to revive the *res publica* and create new civic institutions which can support it, ones on a par with the seventeenth-century churches of Rome. This collage of new and old, utopian syndicalism and traditional city, is characteristic of the European Rationalists in Brussels, Barcelona, Paris and Italy generally.

So far only imperfect fragments of the style and idea have been realised, one on the edge of Paris. Georgia Benamo and Christian de Portzamparc have completed a small urban scheme, the Rue des Hautes-Formes. This inevitably seeks to recreate 'the street, the square, the urban place' but at greater density than in a traditional city. Tower and slab blocks of Modernism are combined and given a Post-Modern formal treatment of cut-out screens à la Moore, false hanging arches to signify entry à la Venturi and a variety of window treatment à la mode. The last is further justified as a method of breaking down the scale and reducing the feeling of being overlooked by a thousand eyes – something that would have resulted from an all-window version. If there are contextualist doubts about this scheme they concern the leaky space, the small size of the piazza and *res publica* and the neutralised relation of solid to void, urban *poché* to monument (the scheme lacks monuments).

A more convincing example of urban contextualism, now under construction, is the museum in Stuttgart by James Stirling. This scheme picks up formal cues from the surrounding context, in this case the height and grain of adjacent buildings and the basic axial relationship to the main street. From this entrance axis it layers a sequence of space frontally and at right angles to movement; as in a Rationalist building the grid is felt conceptually throughout although one is forced to move around it in circles and diagonals. Thus a basic dualism is set up between rectilinear and rotational elements, a binary opposition which heightens the appreciation of other contrasts: in particular the De Stijl words collaged onto the Schinkel grammar.

259

260

261

262 JAMES STIRLING, *Staatsgalerie elevation*, the dualities of plan and function are taken up in the details and ornament. Entrance canopies collage a colourful glass and steel structure, reminiscent of De Stijl, onto a striated masonry background, reminiscent of the existing buildings and Schinkel. This acute opposition, ultimately between the technological and cultural, is then mediated when one realises the canopy is a variant of the traditional entry, the primitive hut.

263 ARATA ISOZAKI, *Fujima Country Club*, 1975, in the primary shape of a black, silent barrel vault, which twists into the form of a metaphysical question-mark, ends with a version of Palladio's Villa Poiana. Why Palladio in a Japanese country-club, it asks? The primary form contrasts with the surrounding environment and the modifications of the Villa Poiana (round columns, thick arch, entrance pillars cut in half) have structural justifications, but the overall question-mark and its green 'period' show the arbitrariness of form, postulated by the Metaphysical School. (M. Arai, *The Japan Architect*).

264 HIROSHI HARA, *Awaze House*, 1972. A strong symmetry with a barrel vault of light down the centre and heavy, defensive forms on the sides giving a strong sense of enclosure. Lighting elements, skylights and furniture are given an hieratic treatment which further reinforces a sense of place and domestic shelter. (H. Hara).

The eclectic language incorporates Romanesque arches for the sculpture court and Egyptian cornices for the painting galleries and these references signify 'museum and art' in a stereotypical way while remaining quite subdued. Indeed the Schinkelesque grammar has an overall rationale in this German context as it signifies 'culture' on a popular level. The virtue of this scheme is to use such obvious clichés with a dramatic inventiveness, one which plays up oppositions between past and present, circle and square. The focus of the museum epitomises this contrast; the circular court is a 'domeless dome', an inside-out space, the room towards which one moves to find oneself outside, cut off from urban noise and in touch with sculpture or the sky. The ideas behind this, the mandala, the 'dome of heaven – the sky', the 'heart of the city' and the circular *res publica* are, as we've seen, key ideas of many Post-Modernists. They

are as much ideas of content as purely architectural ideas and seek to raise, if not answer, metaphysical questions which Modernists, in their pragmatic phase, overlooked.

One could speak of a Metaphysical School of Post-Modernism which loosely unites architects from many different countries, particularly those in America and Japan. Monta Mozuna and Hiroshi Hara use themes of the mandala and 'centred space' which are similar to those of Charles Moore and James Stirling. Hara has written: 'Homogeneous space tends to atomise human relationships . . . if you agree that homogeneous space is negative and undesirable, then we must somehow regain control of the Post-Modern spatial order . . . a house . . . must possess a strong independent centre. This creates a regular order that is opposed to the surrounding homogeneous space outside.'[68] His work, like the others, makes use of strong enclosures, repetitive grids, axial symmetries, mirror images, Palladian motifs and a religious handling of objects. Interior volumes are arranged as so many altars, hieratically fixed on an axis of light which

265 KAZUHIRO ISHII, *Naoshima School*, 1977. A colonnade and other traditional forms such as a pitched roof gate mediate a modern shed space behind. The complicated rhythm of the colonnade (A, B, A, C, A, B, 2A, C, A, C, A, B, 2A, C, A, B, A, C, 2A, C) plays on and syncopates Renaissance examples while other historicist comments include 'missing columns' (indicated by hanging capitals). (K. Ishii).

runs down the spine of the building. They provide the body image and 'heart' which Charles Moore and others have called for in architecture (above, page 113).

More historicist in his metaphysical conceits is Kazuhiro Ishii, an architect who was trained under Moore at Yale. His '54 Windows', a house for a doctor, uses popular signs and colour codes which he argues are regional in nature, or his Naoshima School transforms the Renaissance colonnade into a Post-Modern, syncopated paradox. In the latter building he occasionally leaves out columns thus dealing with the Renaissance 'problem of the corner' in an ironic way. But he orchestrates these Mannerist jokes (hanging capitals of steel bars) with an obviousness that opens the reference out to non-architects.

Michael Graves, by contrast, is less explicit with his humour, as indeed his metaphysics. The work of Graves is coded with a depth and complexity that eludes quick understanding. His Schulman House addition makes use of historicist elements — the ziggurat, the Baroque stagger in plan, the column, entrance 'pediment' and so on — but it changes the scale and colour to distort the perception of these elements sometimes beyond recognition. For instance the decorative moulding over the front door is just barely a pediment and keystone. Graves would argue (above, page 67) that only a distortion of traditional syntax will foreground these elements and decontaminate their potentially kitsch quality, an argument that has some force. And yet at the same time it raises corresponding problems: a certain archness of reference, a lack of focus and unity (which may be intended). Recently Graves has moved towards a more Post-Modern explicitness and one can actually identify certain traditional signs. Not only the elements mentioned but the green of the earth, the blue of the sky and the conventional focii of the house, the hearth and front door. Then as one examines the architecture further, more elaborate cues become apparent. An asymmetrical symmetry on the garden and entrance sides and the presence/absence of columns. This last is another Mannerist paradox. The column has jumped off the centre of the front and landed to one side, or conversely, the

266 MICHAEL GRAVES, *Schulman House*, axonometric from garden shows an ornamental use of the grid applied at different scales to accentuate depth, and the twin centres of door and hearth.

Page 140

267 JAMES WINES and SITE, *Notch Project*, Sacremento, 1977. The metaphysics of 'de-architecture' leads to buildings which peel, crumble or, here, crack open and slide apart. Every morning at nine this forty-five ton wedge moves forty feet to swallow BEST shoppers. Wines has developed many ironic images of an architecture meant to show man that he (and she) lives in an entropic, fragmenting, crumbling, imperfect, ugly, awful universe which is funny. (SITE).

268 KAZUHIRO ISHII, *'54 Windows'*, 1976. This house and office for a doctor incorporates this large number of differing windows to symbolise Japanese regionalism. Ishii argues that a regional quality of 'excess and display' is picked up by the green and orange boxes and other popular signs including the die. The plurality of signs in a grid is also meant to signify urban pluralism. (Anthony Antoniadis).

Page 141

269, 270 MICHAEL GRAVES, *Schulman House*, Princeton, 1976–8. Asymmetrical symmetry is set up on the entrance and garden sides by emphasising both the centre and one side. On the front forms dimish and stagger in plan to emphasise the door. which is further accentuated by decorative 'pediment' and ziggurat. The garden side creates a similar tension between 'off-centre' and 'near-symmetrical sides' and uses fragments of a moulding to also separate signs of sky and ground. The scale disjunctions are a typical Gravesian device to increase interest in traditional forms. (Norman McGrath).

267

268

269

270

capital has jumped off the column-chimney and landed in the centre. Either way it's an amusing, if arcane, architectural conceit.

The question of traditional, applied ornament has started to exercise Post-Modernists with increasing frequency. There have been exhibitions, conferences and magazines on the subject, not to mention countless projects and completed works.[69] It is safe to assume

271 YASUFUMI KAJIMA, *Matsuo Shrine*, 1975–6. A barrel-vaulted temple added onto a traditional Japanese shrine which uses decorative coffers and capitals from the Western tradition to contrast with Eastern ornament. The small scale and precision mouldings increase the hallucinatory quality. Ornament here acts as a classifier of mood, to accentuate the meditative atmosphere. (Y. Kajima).

272 THOMAS GORDON SMITH, *Matthews Street House project*, 1978. Picking up cues from the context, 'the painted ladies of San Francisco', and nineteenth-century polychromatic experiments, this house uses decorative detail ironically (the 'ruin column missing from the front') and semantically (to distinguish formal front from informal back). This aedicular treatment of the entrance is conventional in California bungalows. (T. G. Smith).

that ornament will flourish again soon, purged of its connection with 'crime' and other guilt-laden associations, to fulfill many of its traditional roles. These include not only the symbolic functions which Venturi and Stern have underlined but more obviously aesthetic ones: to give scale, depth and proportion to large, bureaucratic monoliths; to provide variation on themes stated elsewhere in the building and to highlight these; to 'hide faults in construction', something which Modernism in its more Calvinistic moments wanted to show; to give enjoyment, complication and visual games to a boring surface, and finally to accent the mood of a space rather the way spice and garlic accentuate taste. When Modernism cut ornament from the diet of architecture a lot more than bad taste was purged, and it is one of the pleasures of Post-Modernism to bring back these delicacies one by one.

Hans Hollein, already adept at the slick-tech look of Late-Modernism, has turned his attention towards the ornamental use of this aesthetic. In his renovation of the Perchtoldsdorf Townhall, near Vienna, he has produced a grand, ornamental use of chrome and furniture elements to intensify the existing ornament. Here an undulating blue line edged in chrome divides the wall in parts above the traditional dado line, in order to accentuate the existing portraits of the previous mayors. The waves vary in breadth, as do the rippling panels below, to conform with the varying ovals of the paintings above. Over the side entrance doors, otherwise unarticulated except for handles, the waves invert to allow headroom and signal a change of function. This contextual use of ornament (reminiscent of Viennese Rococo) signifies a positive functional choice Hollein made when confronted with the difficult requirement of adding to the size of the council chamber. He decided that rather than building a new chamber he would crowd all the councillors into the old one and thereby preserve their historic link with a room that has great emotional overtones (the commemorative portraits were painted soon after a Turkish deception that resulted in the massacre of the town's people). The crowded ornament thus not only half frames the elders, but also half frames the crowded councillors seated below, and thus acts as a metaphorical link between the two. The latter are squashed tight against each other in thin, Art Deco chairs which just fit into places allotted at the table. On the floor in the centre of the oval is a stylised vine and bunch of grapes, a symbol both of the major source of revenue of this town and (because of the golden marble lumps) money itself.

In scale and concept, Hollein's designs are midway between architecture and furniture and thus lend themselves to ornamental treatment. His Austrian Travel Agency in Vienna consists of an ornamental series of giant furniture-pieces juxtaposed as a symbolic collage. On the exterior the neutral, grey urban fabric is preserved and yet the new function is subtly cued by the introduction of polished bronze which gleams out from it. On the inside the various tourist fantasies, and stereotypes, become an excuse for an eclecticism I would once again term Radical because of its semantic appropriateness: ruined columns impaled by chrome shafts signify travel in Greece and Italy; desert travel is communicated by bronze versions of the palm columns at the Brighton Pavilion; India by a bronze solartopee, theatre tickets by a stage curtain, air travel by birds and, ironically, the place where one pays for it all, the cashier's desk, is

271
272
276
277
275
273
274

273 HANS HOLLEIN, *Austrian Travel Agency*, axonometric, shows the symbolic centres collaged onto an abstract grid of space with circles, staggers and rise and fall of section articulating the zones between selling (above) and private work areas (top). Continuous open space is thus characterised and dramatised, as opposed to Late-Modern isotropic space.

274 HANS HOLLEIN, *Austrian Travel Agency*, Vienna, 1976–8. The cashiers' desks are Rolls-Royce radiator grills, in substance. Stereotypes are both explicit and distorted by the luxuriant materials and precision craftsmanship. (J. Surwillo).

signified by the outlines of a Rolls Royce radiator grill. All of this is sheltered under a light-filled coffered vault reminiscent of the local Post Office Savings Bank, the magnificent 'Modern' space Otto Wagner built in 1906. Thus local reference is set against stereotype, and existing urban fabric against infill. Because of the precision craftsmanship the stereotypes, like those of Dixon and Stirling mentioned previously, avoid becoming kitsch. Hollein thus speaks directly to a mass-culture and uses its clichés (something of a necessity in a travel bureau) – but with a wit and care not usually evident in the products of mass-culture.

The way architecture communicates with this industrial society has to be seen as a major challenge for Post-Modernism. Clearly Modernism failed to speak to this society in several of the ways outlined at the beginning of this book. Just as clearly Post-Modernists such as Robert Venturi have been equivocal about engaging this issue. Wrapped up in the problem are various questions which make a simple approach to it impossible – such as the balance between populist and elite codes, both of which architects have to serve, and their attendant threats of kitsch and mystification. Furthermore there are the problems of a consumer society which celebrates private building and not public architecture. The architect, presuming he wishes to communicate positively with this society through his building, must steer a circuitous course through these obstacles. To reiterate, he must appeal to different taste cultures using different codes, and this will make him an eclectic. Whether he produces weak or Radical Eclecticism depends on whether he finds compelling reasons for using a style. Simplifying somewhat we can point to three basic justifications for choosing a style, or mixing them, as the case may be: the context that the building fits into, the character of the particular functions which must be enhanced by style and the taste-culture of the inhabitants. We can see these three aspects in Charles Moore's half-completed Piazza d'Italia in New Orleans.

As the aerial view of the urban context reveals, this piazza is set in a mixed area of New Orleans. To one side

Page 144
275 HANS HOLLEIN, *Perchtoldsdorf Townhall*, renovation, Austria, 1975–6. The wavy decorative lines in blue and chrome mediate between the ceiling, table and floor ornament while the stylised vine and grapes provide visual distraction during interminable debates. An old doorway is kept while the two side doorways are subtly cued by an inversion of the wave. A sympathetic collage of old and new which has a semantic justification. (J. Surwillo).

276, 277 HANS HOLLEIN, *Perchtoldsdorf Townhall*. View towards the mayor's seat showing decorative vine and wavy line below existing portraits of the mayors painted in the 1690s. The table and chairs are really a giant architectural element which gives permanence and solemnity to the public realm. From the mayor's chair the black acoustic panels are designed to all appear democratically the same, equal to one vote. (J. Surwillo).

Page 145
278, 279 HANS HOLLEIN, *Austrian Travel Agency*, Vienna, 1976–8. Placed under the cool white light of a Secessionist barrel vault, which subtly mediates between different ceiling heights, are various signs of foreign travel: a bronze Lutyens dome for India, palm trees for exotic places, a ruined column for Greece and Italy, a truncated pyramid (in the corners) for Egypt. Air flight is signalled by birds, boat travel by ships' railing and theatre tickets by curtain and Serlian 'comic scene'.

274

275

276

277

278

279

is a Modern skyscraper, the black and white graphics of which have been taken up as a motif to generate a graduating series of rings. This circular form, at once a Modern 'bull's-eye' and Baroque urban form (Place des Victoires, Paris), permeates out into three streets giving a cue to the passer-by that something unusual occurs behind the existing buildings. This setting up of an expectation, and the use of veiling devices that at once proclaim and hide — the archway, the pergola — dramatise the approach. We are pulled towards the centre of the bull's-eye and expect to find there a symmetrical, circular culmination. What actually occurs both satisfies and contradicts this supposition. There are indeed a centre and circular forms, but instead of them confirming a Baroque centrality, they set up new expectancies. The circles are partial discs, screens of columns that spin asymmetrically on the diagonal of movement towards a new culmination point, the tallest point, an archway, in fact a Modern *Serliana*. This diagonal is reinforced by the cascade of broken forms — the boot of Italy — which focuses on the highest plateau, the 'Italian Alps'. Thus we have a clear organisation of form and content. As Italy rises towards the Northern Alps, so too do the Five Orders of Italian columns, and they culminate in a new sixth order which frames the future restaurant. This invention for a German restaurant (they will hang sausages in the windows) Moore calls the 'Deli Order'. Neon necklaces around the neck of these columns further indicate that this is the twentieth century and that commercial bad taste is a part of it. Moore has a liking for architectural whimsy and puns (he calls his watering metopes 'wetopes') and it is a credit to his teamwork that these calculated lapses in taste don't get the upper hand. They are part of a rich mix of meanings rather the way similar elements are absorbed into Shakespearean drama.

A point worth stressing is that the plurality of meanings in this scheme could not have been successfully incorporated by one designer (a point to be made generally about participation, see above pages 104–5). Moore has teamed up with two local architects from the firm of Perez and Associates and these designers supplied much of the peculiar cultural knowledge. They were the ones to stress the importance of the annual St. Joseph's festival, the pretext for the fountain and piazza. Once a year the Italian community comes to the fore to celebrate its presence and they do so by selling Italian specialities and local concoctions (muffalattas, salami, cheese, etc) on the day of their patron saint. Since the ostensible reason for the piazza was to give identity to the Italian community in a city where other ethnic groups dominate (the French, Spanish, the blacks and Anglos) there was a sufficient pretext for historicist rhetoric and explicit content. What was the content? 'Italianess' clearly as symbolised by the echoes of the Trevi fountain, the Five rather than Three Orders, the strong earth colouring, the Latin inscription ('This fountain was given by the citizens of New Orleans as a gift to all the people') and most obviously the plan of Italy (with the Adriatic and Tyrrhenian seas represented by moving water). Since the community is made up mostly of Sicilians this island occupies the centre of the bull's-eye, an emphasis which is increased by another focus, the black and white podium. This can function as a speaker's platform on St. Joseph's day when the piazza works as a *res publica*. This particular function is the kind of detailed social content that emerges as a possibility

only after patient exploration into a local culture, and it gives the rhetorical forms a credibility they would otherwise lack. But it is a rhetoric that extends across many taste-cultures.

For historians there are references to the Marine Theatre of Hadrian and the triumphal gateways of Schinkel; for the Sicilians there are references to archetypal piazzas and fountains; for the Modernists there is an acknowledgement of skyscrapers and the use of current technologies (the neon and concrete); for the lover of pure architectural form there are cutaway imposts finished in speckled marble and a most sensuous use of polished stainless steel. Column capitals glisten with this material as water shoots out of the acanthus leaves; or the stern, squat Tuscan columns are cut from this material leaving razor-sharp 'paramilitary' images, the silhouettes of Greek helmets.[70] The overall impression finally is a sensuous and rhetorical one, perhaps a bit too overemphasised at present because its background infill isn't finished. But conceptually it is a convincing example of Radical Eclecticism: it fits into and extends the urban context, it characterises the various functions, symbolic and practical, with various styles, and it takes its cues for content and form from the local taste-culture, the Italian community. Moreover it provides this community with a centre, a 'heart', to repeat the Post-Modern catchword. While engaging a mass-culture with recognised stereotypes, it manages to use them *both* straightforwardly and in an inventive, distorted way. Finally, and on a predictive note, it foreshadows an architecture like the Baroque, when different arts were combined together to produce a rhetorical whole. Clearly the success of this rhetoric depends on an area outside of architecture: the belief in a credible social or metaphysical content. The search for such content is the next challenge for Post-Modernists.

Page 148
280 CHARLES MOORE (with Allen Eskew and Malcolm Heard Jr. of Perez & Associates and Ron Filson), *Piazza d'Italia*, New Orleans, 1976–9. The aerial view shows the piazza (circle) set into the urban tissue (rectangle) like a mandala which announces its presence by various cues: a pergola, a campanile and archway or the rings of paving. This scheme, like many Rationalist ones, seeks to reinforce the historic urban fabric while at the same time changing its meaning. (U.I.G.).

281 *Piazza d'Italia*, Tuscan Order to right is 'fluted' with water jets; Doric to left has 'Wetopes' and Moore's face spitting out water; in back are Composite (left) and Corinthian (right) while the boot of Italy is perceived as a cascade of black and white strata.

Page 149
282 *Piazza d'Italia*, Doric Order above Sardinia, although proportioned on Vignola, breaks several rules. The dark, wet glistening steel has been given a paramilitary image of a Greek helmet; imposts of veined marble again resemble rendered cross-sections.

283 *Piazza d'Italia*, view from above shows screen discs whirling about the centre, Sicily, while opening towards the North, the Alps. Traditional forms are broken but still remain.

284 *Piazza d'Italia*, pergola entrance temple is both straightforward in lettering and relationships and distorted: it is skewed in plan to conform to the pie-shape, thus giving a perspective effect, and the proportions are more slender than usual due to the new materials of open pipe-work and concrete.

280

283

281

cover

NOTES

1 See Mies van der Rohe, 'Industrialized Building', originally printed in the magazine, *G*, Berlin, 1924, and reprinted in Ulrich Conrads, *Programmes and Manifestoes on 20th-Century Architecture*, London, 1970, p. 81.

2 See Manfredo Tafuri, 'L'Architecture dans le boudoir', *Oppositions 3*, New York, 1974, p. 45 and note p. 60. Tafuri claims that the 'accusations of fascism hurled at Rossi mean little, since his attempts at the recovery of an ahistoricizing form exclude verbalizations of its content and any compromise with the real'. This escape clause is of course impossible; all form will be looked at historically and have conventional associations tied to it, and Rossi's work cannot escape this 'compromise with the real' any more than all other architecture.

3 Peter and Alison Smithson, *Architectural Design*, October 1969, p. 560.

4 Peter Smithson, *Architectural Design*, May 1975, p. 272.

5 A. et P. Smithson, 'Gentle Cultural Accommodation', *L'Architecture d'aujourd'hui*, Janvier/Février 1975, pp. 4–13, quote from page 9. The Smithsons contend that they didn't write this, although it is typical of their ideas. See *Architectural Design* 7, 1977 and my answer.

6 See Tom Wolfe, *The New Journalism*, Picador, London, 1975, pp. 54–6, and my article 'The Rise of Post-Modern Architecture', *Architectural Association Quarterly*, London, Summer 1976, pp. 7–14.

7 For the call to morality see Sigfried Giedion, *Space, Time and Architecture*, Cambridge, Mass., 1971, pp. 214, 291–308. For the 'Heroic Period', see Peter and Alison Smithson, issue of *Architectural Design*, December 1965.

8 Sant' Elia's 'Manifesto', July 11, 1914, is quoted from *Futurismo 1909–1919*, exhibition of Italian Futurism, organised by Northern Arts and the Scottish Arts Council, 1972, catalogue, p. 49.

9 A more rigorous comparison of architecture to language is made by architectural semioticians, who substitute technical terms for these imprecise analogues. For our general purpose however, the analogies will suffice, as long as we don't take them too literally.

10 A point made by Umberto Eco in 'Function and Sign: Semiotics and Architecture', published in *Structures Implicit and Explicit*, Graduate School of Fine Arts University of Pennsylvania, Vol. 2, 1973. Republished in our anthology edited by Geoffrey Broadbent, Dick Bunt and myself, *Signs, Symbols and Architecture*, Wiley, to appear in 1978.

11 See Umberto Eco, 'A Componential Analysis of the Architectural Sign/Column', in *Semiotica 5*, Number 2, 1972, Mouton, The Hague, pp. 97–117.

12 See for instance Herbert Gans' description of the five major 'taste cultures' in his *Popular Culture and High Culture*, Basic Books, New York, 1974, pp. 69–103.

13 See G. L. Hersey, 'J. C. Loudon and Architectural Associationism', *Architectural Review*, August, 1968, pp. 89–92.

14 The use of 'naturally' begs the important semiotic issue of exactly *how* natural a sign can be. They all depend on coding, and therefore convention. But the issue is too complex to be treated here. See Umberto Eco, *A Theory of Semiotics*, Indiana University Press, Bloomington, 1976, pp. 191–221.

15 I've discussed these debates in *Modern Movements in Architecture*, Harmondsworth & New York, 1973, pp. 318–28, and footnotes for references. The Italian press took up the controversy and applied the metaphors of 'refrigeration' to English criticism (if my memory serves me).

16 Philip Johnson, 'The Seven Crutches of Modern Architecture,' *Perspecta* III, New Haven, 1955; 'Whence and Whither', The Processional Element in Architecture, *Perspecta* 9/10, New Haven, 1965.

17 See John Jacobus, *Philip Johnson*, George Braziller, New York, 1962.

18 Letter to Jurgen Joedicke, 6/12/1961 reprinted in John Jacobus: *Philip Johnson*, New York, 1962.

19 See Robin Boyd, *New Directions in Japanese Architecture*, New York and London, 1968, p. 102.

20 See *CIAM '59 in Otterlo*, ed. Jurgen Joedicke, London, 1961, p. 182.

21 A fairly complete bibliography of these writings and comment on the Venturi Team can be seen in *Learning from Las Vegas*, revised edition by Robert Venturi, Denise Scott Brown and Steven Izenour, Cambridge, 1977. For a criticism see my review, 'Venturi et. al. are almost all right', in *Architectural Design*, 7, 1977.

22 See *Learning from Las Vegas, op. cit.*, pp. 130 & 149.

23 They have often pointed this out; Robert Venturi for instance said at a conference at Art Net, London, July 1976: 'I apologise for all these Rich Men's houses, but I'll take anything we can get'. Their projects are often for more social tasks, sometimes minority groups and the under-serviced.

24 See *A & U, 74 : 11* devoted to their work from 1970–74, p. 43.

25 See my 'MBM and the Barcelona School', *The Architectural Review*, March 1977, pp. 159–65, and *Arquitectura Bis, 13 & 14*, Barcelona, May–June, 1976.

26 I've discussed this 'threat' of pluralism and eclecticism in 'Isozaki and Radical Eclecticism', *Architectural Design*, January, 1977, pp. 42–8. In this article I try to distinguish between a radical eclecticism which is semantically based and multivalent and the nineteenth-century 'weak eclecticism' which was an easy-going shuffling of styles.

27 I am investigating this partly in *Ersatz – The International Culture of Our Time* to appear in 1979.

28 See Aldo Rossi, *L'Architettura della Citta*, Padua, 1966. *Arquitecturas Bis*, No. 12, pp. 25–31. Gijon is a monumental form of classicism with Venturi-like juxtapositions.

29 See *L'Architecture d'Aujourd'hui*, the issue devoted to *Formalisme-Realisme*, 190, April, 1977, p. 101.

30 I'm sure there will be misunderstandings on this score as I seem to be having it both ways, arguing in favour of 'the spirit of the age' and against it; but the distinctions between 'climate of opinion' and 'Zeitgeist' concern the former's basis in convention not necessity, choice not force, change not permanence, morality not behaviour.

31 Henry-Russell Hitchcock, *Architecture Nineteenth & Twentieth Centuries*, Harmondsworth, Penguin edition, 1971, p. 533.

32 Quinlan Terry, 'Architectural Renaissance', *Building Design*, Sept. 17, 1976, p. 18. Terry gave a lecture in a series on Post-Modernism at the AA in 1976.

33 For an excellent discussion, of this trend, see Chris Fawcett, 'An Anarchist's Guide to Modern Architecture', *AAQ*, no. 7, vol. 3, 1975, pp. 37–57. The 'guide' is not so much about anarchism as parody.

34 Conrad Jameson's writings have mostly been published in England, in various journals. Among the sources are: 'Social Research in Architecture', *The Architects Journal*, 27 October, 1971, and following controversy; 'Architect's Error', *New Society*, 8 May, 1975, and following controversy; 'Enter Pattern Books, Exit Public Housing Architects: a friendly sermon'. *The Architects Journal*, 11 February 1976, and following controversy; 'British Architecture: Thirty Wasted Years', *The Sunday Times*, February, 1977, and following controversy. Jameson, unlike other polemicists, really knows how to fire the nerve-ends of modern architects. His book *Notes for a Revolution in Urban Planning*, will be published by Penguin and Harpers Row, sometime in 1978.

280

281

282

283

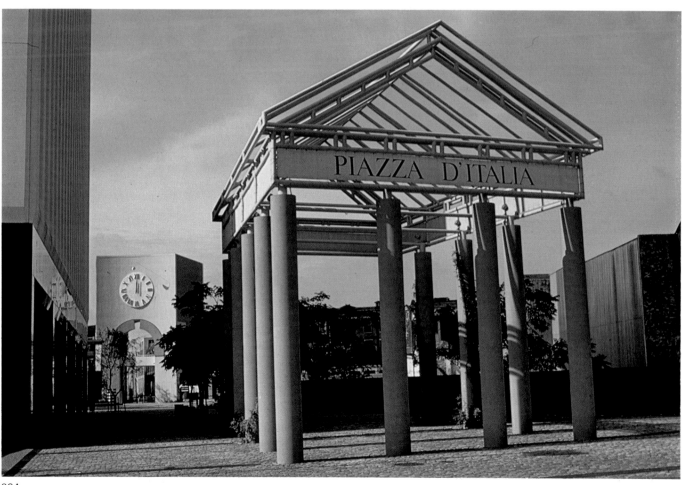

284

35 Maurice Culot, one leader of ARAU in Brussels, spent ten days at Port Grimaud discussing its implications with the architect Francois Spoerry. In conversation, June, 1977, he told me he was convinced this was the type of housing for the people, but that his local Communist leaders, some attuned to 1930s models, might not accept this.

36 David Gebhardt, 'Getty's Museum', *Architecture Plus*, Sept./Oct., 1974, pp. 57–60, 122. See also Reyner Banham, 'The Lair of the Looter', *New Society*, 5 May, 1977, p. 238; Building Design, Sept. 13, 1974; In England, *The Observer* and *Times* ran articles on the building.

37 James Stirling, letter in *Oppositions*, 1976, Summer, p. 130. But some part of Stirling's recent work is definitely Post-Modern in its Contextualism – his Dusseldorf and Cologne projects, see below.

38 Colin Amery and Lance Wright, 'Lifting the Witches Curse', *The Architecture of Darbourne and Darke*, RIBA Publications, 17 May– 29 July 1977, exhibition handbook, pp. 7–8.

39 Andrew Derbyshire, 'Building the Welfare State', *RIBA Conference 1976*, RIBA Publications, *op. cit.*, p. 29.

40 Ibid, p. 50.

41 Aldo Van Eyck, 'In Search of Labyrinthian Clarity', *L'Architecture d'Aujourd'hui*, Jan/Feb, 1975, p. 18.

42 *RIBA Conference, op. cit.*, p. 62.

43 The 1968 Skeffington Report recommended greater public participation in planning, but so far this has led only to increased consultation, or the minimum choice about room layout, location of partitions, etc., as in the PSSHAK project, or to the development of plans, as in the Swinbrook project of North Kensington.

44 'Signification and richness' in architecture are assumed as ultimate values in my argument, and not justified here; arguments for pluralism in politics are given by Karl Popper, for richness in art by I. A. Richards. For my misgivings concerning the Neo-Rationalists, see 'The Irrational Rationalists', *A & U*, April and May, 1977, to be published in *The Rationalists*, ed. Dennis Sharp, Architectural Press, London 1978.

45 See *Architectural Design*, No. 3, 1977, p. 191, the issue devoted to Culot, Krier and Tafuri.

46 Hannah Arendt has written about the public realm at length in *The Human Condition*, Chicago, 1958; *On Revolution*, New York, 1963. Her ideas have influenced George Baird, Ken Frampton, Conrad Jameson, Nikolaus Habraken among others in the field of architecture.

47 Leo Krier, 'A City with a City', *Architectural Design*, No. 3, 1977, p. 207.

48 See Grahame Shane, 'Contextualism', *Architectural Design*, No. 11, 1976, pp. 676–9, for a discussion and bibliography.

49 Colin Rowe, 'Collage City', *The Architectural Review*, August, 1975, p. 80.

50 *Ibid.*, pp. 80–81.

51 See Nathan Silver's letter to *The Architectural Review*, Sept., 1975, and following exchanges.

52 See T. S. Eliot, *After Strange Gods*, London 1934.

53 Kent C. Bloomer and Charles W. Moore, *Body, Memory and Architecture*, Yale University Press, New Haven, 1977, p. 41–2.

54 Carl G. Jung, *et al, Man and his Symbols*, Aldus Books, London, 1964, p. 78.

55 See Rudolf Wittkower, *Studies in the Italian Baroque*, London and New York. 1975, p. 63.

56 For the notions of layering see Colin Rowe and Robert Slutsky, 'Literal and Phenomenal Transparency', *Perspecta 8*, 13–14; for 'compaction composition' see my *Le Corbusier and the Tragic View of Architecture*, London and Cambridge, 1973.

57 Robert Stern has written on Post-Modernism in various journals, among them *Architectural Design*, 4, 1977, and has defined three aspects to it: contextualism, historical allusion and applied ornament. In America the social and participatory aspects of PM are considered unimportant as the argument is conducted more on the stylistic and semantic levels. Stern has discussed 'inclusivism' in his *New Directions in American Architecture*, New York and London, 1969, re-edited with a postscript on Post-Modern, 1977.

58 C. Ray Smith, Supermannerism, *New Attitudes in Post-Modern Architecture*, E. P. Dutton, New York, 1977, pp. 91–9.

59 See Maggie Keswick, *Chinese Gardens*, New York and London, 1978. The last chapter, which I wrote, discusses the notion of this kind of liminal, religious space, a notion which I adapted from Edmund Leach's concepts. See his *Culture and Communication*, Cambridge, 1976, pp. 14, 51, 71–5, 86–7.

60 See Charles Moore, 'Hadrian's Villa', *Perspecta 6*, 1958, 'You Have to Pay for the Public Life', *Perspecta 9/10*, 1975, both reprinted in *Dimensions*, with Gerald Allen, New York, 1977. See also the issue of *Architecture d'Aujourd'hui*, March/April, 1976.

61 *Architecture d'Aujourd'hui*, ibid., p. 60.

62 The idea has not been developed here, but see, for instance, Juan Pablo Bonta, 'Notes for a Theory of Design', in *Versus, 6*, Milano, 1974. If meaning consists in relation then a restricted as well as rich palette can articulate it. My general favouring of rich over restricted systems is partly due to our Miesian age, and partly due to the fact that elites and specialists are better at decoding restricted systems than the general public.

63 See Basil Bernstein, *Class, Codes and Control*, Vols. I & II, London, 1971–3 and Linda Clarke, 'Explorations into the nature of environmental codes', the *Journal of Architectural Research*, Vol. 3, No. 1, 1974.

64 The studies are admittedly very fragmentary and made with students in England, Norway and California, although several interviews at buildings were conducted in England and Holland. One study has been published, 'A Semantic Analysis of Stirling's Olivetti Centre Wing', in *AAQ*, Vol. 6, no. 2, 1974, and part of another is included in my 'Architectural Sign' which will be published in *Signs, Symbols and Architecture*, the anthology edited by Richard Bunt, Geoffrey Broadbent and myself. Supporting evidence can be found in B. Bernstein, *op. cit.* and Philip Boudon, *Lived-in Architecture Le Corbusier's Pessac revisited*, London 1972, pp. 46, 65, 112.

65 See chapter 3, *Late-Modern Architecture*, Selected Essays, Academy, London and Rizzoli, New York, 1980.

66 The Chicago Seven were formed in 1976 partly in response to other city groupings. By the time of the Townhouse competition, March 1978, they included eleven architects: Thomas Beeby, Laurence Booth, Stuart Cohen, James Freed, Gerald Horn, Helmut Jahn, James Nagle, Kenneth Schroeder, Stanley Tigerman, Cynthia Weese and Ben Weese.

67 See 'Roma Interrotta', *Architectural Design*, Vol. 49, Nos 3/4, 1979, p. 163.

68 'Hiroshi Hara an Interview with David Stewart', *AAQ*, Vol. 10, No. 4, 1978, pp. 8, 10.

69 See Stephen Kieran, *VIA III* On Ornament, Penn., 1977; a symposium at the Architectural Association in Dec. 1978 on 'The Question of Ornament' (unpublished); Boyd Auger, 'A Return to Ornament', *The Architectural Review*, 1976 and subsequent correspondence; an exhibition at the Cooper-Hewitt Museum organised by Richard Oliver, 1978; E. H. Gombrich, *The Sense of Order*, a study in the psychology of decorative art, Phaidon, Oxford, 1979.

70 Several of these meanings were pointed out to me by Charles Moore in a discussion, March 1979; others can be found in Martin Filler's excellent article on the Piazza in *Progressive Architecture*, Nov. 1978, pp. 81–7.

INDEX